The Official Cub Scout Annual
of The Scout Association

Scouts

Edited by Peter Brooks

This book belongs to

Andrew Mitchell

Name of Pack

11 Forth Valley Cubs

KT-578-731

Contents

£4·35

Cliff Brown's Communications Puzzle Page

Check your answers on page 59

GARDEN BIRD-SPOT

It's great watching birds. It doesn't matter where you live, if you look out of your window you will see some kind of bird. What's more, they're not all sparrows or starlings, or gulls flying over on their way to the local rubbish tip. Look closer and you will find that there are many different species that regularly visit a garden.

Between October and March these garden birds need our help. Food and water can be hard to find in winter, but if we put out wild bird food and kitchen scraps, and provide ice-free water, we will be helping to keep many of these garden visitors alive.

Here are some of the garden birds which you should look out for.

Starling – usually arrives in noisy flocks. Males and females look alike. Because this bird is very "spotty" and has a dark bill, we can tell that it is in winter plumage. By spring many of the spots will have worn away and the bill will have become yellow.

House sparrow – this is a male. The females are much duller with fainter marks. They eat many different types of food, but the strong bill is well suited to feeding on seeds.

Blue tit – many people's favourite. Away from gardens they will feed on small seeds hanging from thin branches. In gardens they will feed from hanging peanut dispensers. Usually only a few come at one time, but during a day a large number, a hundred or more, may pass through one town garden.

Song thrush – often very shy, but quite common, even in towns. Its repetitive song may sometimes be heard during mild winter days. It seldom visits bird-tables, but hunts for worms and feeds on fruit and berries.

Chaffinch – this is the colourful male. The female is much duller, rather like a sparrow but with bold white wing bars. In a national survey, members of the Young Ornithologists' Club found chaffinches to be much more common in gardens in Scotland, Ireland and Wales than in England, especially in the south east of England where they were very few.

Great tit – larger than the blue tit with a black stripe down its breast. Males have thicker stripes than females. They like to feed on hanging food, but often feed on the ground as well. It's a bossy bird which will often chase other smaller birds away.

Greenfinch – males are more colourful than females. The birds' bodies are green, but the flashes in the wings and tail are yellow. The big thick bill shows that their natural food is seed.

Blackbird – most gardens have a resident blackbird. Males are black and females are brown. They may be seen catching worms on the grass or turning over leaves under bushes as they look for small creatures to eat.

Robin – both male and female robins look alike. They are one of the few birds to sing all through the year, even in the middle of winter. They sing because they want to keep their own territories and they are never seen in flocks.

Dunnock – perhaps the most secretive and overlooked garden bird, yet most gardens have one or two. It rarely visits a bird-table, but looks for food on the grass or under bushes, moving with mouse-like jerks or flicking its wings nervously.

You can help birds even more by joining the Young Ornithologists' Club, junior section of The Royal Society for the Protection of Birds.

If you would like to receive information about this special club for young people interested in birds and wildlife then write to YOC, The Lodge, SANDY, Bedfordshire SG19 2DL. Please remember to enclose a second class stamp.

The **1990 Cub Scout Annual** extends its thanks to Peter Holden, of The Royal Society for the Protection of Birds, for his help in the production of this feature. The photographs are the work of: M.W. Richards; C.H. Gomersall; R. Wilmshurst; J.L. Roberts; P.R. Perfect; S. & B.A. Craig and J. Markham and were supplied by the RSPB's Photographic Library.

The Great MECCANO Wordsearch Competition

50 FIRST PRIZES

Hidden in the word-square are the 52 animals and insects which are listed here. They run horizontally, diagonally and vertically, forwards and backwards. When you have found them all, there will be 55 letters left that you have not used – these, read in order, will give you the names of *six* more animals and insects.

When you have found the missing six, fill them in on the coupon below the grid, send it in to the address shown and *you* could be one of our *50* First Prize winners.

Each of the lucky 50 will receive a fantastic Meccano No. 4 kit – quality construction sets, designed to the highest specifications and supplied with a detailed instruction booklet to show you just how versatile these kits can be.

The prizes for this competition have been generously donated by Meccano.

Don't miss our other great competition on pages 54 and 55 in this Annual – **and remember** you can send both competition entry coupons in the same envelope and we'll sort them out!

```
D L E M A C T T R F R O G A O M
E I B G M O A D A O E R G Y P H
R O H O A C I S N X D O I C E E
E N U D A K R P S N I H P L O D
R S Q U I R R E L O P S S L U G
E N R M V O L E G R S U A U S E
E A S O H A O H V P M P N E R H
D K G L H C L S B A D G E R O O
O E L E P H A N T W E T A W O G
F L Y O M O R O A M G B A C R I
S A E R N G P G E R B I L O A R
N H O T W O C I P I B E W D G A
A W A S P N E W T I G E R R N F
I E A P O L A R B E A R Z K A F
L N I P L L A E S A T Y L P K E
T H A M S T E R U S Y E K N O D
```

ANT	**APE**	**HEDGEHOG**	**HIPPOPOTAMUS**
(not part of elephant)	**BADGER**	**HOG** ✓	**HORSE**
ASS	**BEE**	(not part of hedgehog)	**LION**
BEAVER	**CAMEL**	**KANGAROO**	**MOUSE**
BOAR	**COCKROACH**	**MOLE**	**PIG**
CAT	**DEER**	**NEWT**	**RABBIT**
COW	**DOLPHIN**	**POLARBEAR**	**SHEEP**
DOG	**EARWIG**	**SEAL**	**SNAKE**
DONKEY	**ELK**	**SNAIL**	**SPIDER**
ELEPHANT	**FOX**	**SLUG**	**TIGER**
FLY	**GERBIL**	**SQUIRREL**	**VOLE**
FROG	**GNU**	**TOAD**	**WHALE**
GIRAFFE	**HAMSTER**	**WASP**	**ZEBRA**
GOAT		**WORM**	

Detach this coupon and send it (to arrive no later than February 28, 1990) to:

The 1990 Cub Scout Annual Competitions,
Editorial Department,
The Scout Association,
Baden-Powell House,
Queen's Gate,
LONDON
SW7 5JS

The six hidden animals and insects are:
1. _ _ _ _ _ _ _ _ _ (9)
2. _ _ _ _ _ _ _ _ _ _ (10)
3. _ _ _ _ _ _ _ _ _ _ _ (11)
4. _ _ _ _ _ _ _ _ (8)
5. _ _ _ _ _ _ _ _ _ (9)
6. _ _ _ _ _ _ _ _ (8)

Your name and address: (Please use capital letters)

....

.... Post code: ....

I am a Member of the .... Cub Scout Pack

FIVE OF THE BEST!

by David Easton

Courage shows itself in many ways. We expect courage to be shown by the emergency services – the Police, Fire Brigade, Ambulance Service, Lifeboats, Coastguard, Mountain Rescue and so on – and take their many courageous acts for granted. However, when it applies to others who are not normally expected to be courageous, that act of bravery seems, somehow, to be even more special.

Throughout the years Scouting has had many acts of courage recognised and, each year, more and more are added to the list of those special people who show courage in its many forms.

There are those who perform courageous acts of bravery, often without thought to their own safety or well-being. There are those who display tremendous courage despite severe illness or handicap.

Each act, in itself, is an example of living up to the motto of Cub Scouts everywhere, 'Do your best', and here we tell the stories of five Cub Scouts who represent that 'best'!

Jonathan Murden, 9, of the 1st Porchester Cub Scouts, helped drag his disabled grandfather from a blazing house. He and a neighbour battled through thick smoke in the semi-detached house to rescue his normally wheelchair-bound grandfather, who had managed to drag himself into the hall before losing consciousness.

Jonathan got a pillow and blanket from his own bed and stayed with his badly burned grandfather until the ambulance arrived.

Jonathan was awarded the Silver Cross for his bravery.

Jonathan Murden

Stephen Davis, 10, of the 4th Kendal Cub Scouts in Cumbria, rescued his younger brother, Simon, 6, from drowning.

Stephen, a good swimmer, went for an early-morning swim in a pool close to the flat where the family was staying on holiday. Simon, who did not swim and needed to wear armbands while in the water, asked if he could go, too. His parents said they would take him but that he had to wait until they had changed.

His mother thought that Simon was with his father and his father believed that he was with his mother but Simon had gone on his own to the pool. His parents ran to the pool and found Stephen attending to Simon at the poolside.

Stephen had been coming back when Simon passed him on the way to the pool and, instead of coming back to tell his parents, Stephen returned to the pool and found Simon splashing about in trouble in the deep end. Stephen jumped in and hauled his brother on to the side and, in so doing, saved Simon's life.

Stephen was awarded the Medal for Meritorious Conduct for his prompt action.

Stephen Davis

Now for courage of a different kind

Gary Little, 8, of the 16th Tynemouth (St. Augustins), had a terrible experience when he was attacked and savaged by a dog.

He was playing on a beach when a bull terrier ran up and bit him on his leg. His father ran to the scene and managed to pull the dog off but, later, Gary tripped and fell and the dog went for him again, biting his jaw and ear, just missing the jugular vein.

He needed surgery, had 20 stitches inserted and had a 24-hour stay in hospital but, during that time, he impressed both the Police and the hospital consultant with his courage and attitude which, in turn, helped his parents at a very distressing time.

Gary was awarded the Medal for Meritorious Conduct for his courage.

Gary Little

Greg Etheridge, 10, of the 1st Church Hill Cub Scout Pack from Hereford and Worcester, has suffered from spina bifida since birth. He wears calipers on both legs and uses sticks.

Despite these enormous physical problems, Greg is extremely enthusiastic and refuses to give in to his disabilities. He joins in every game – no matter how strenuous – and never asks for special treatment.

His enthusiasm is an inspiration to all and his only regret is that Cub Scout Meetings don't last for seven days a week! He has truly earned his Bronze, Silver and Gold Arrows despite prolonged periods in hospital and, at times, being in great pain.

Greg was awarded the Cornwell Scout Badge in recognition of his outstanding courage.

Greg Etheridge

Andrew Newick

Andrew Newick, 10, of the 3rd Brampton (St. Thomas) Cub Scout Pack in Derbyshire, was found to be suffering from cancer of the lymph gland in 1986. Treatment commenced with surgery and then chemotherapy.

Despite the fact that the treatment, which was initially for ten weeks, caused him to be sick for long periods of time, he was very brave and never complained. The treatment caused a big weight loss and continued every three weeks until mid-June.

During his treatment, Andrew took part in a sponsored fun-run and, by both walking and running, raised £580 for Sheffield Children's Hospital. He also took part in two weekend camps, a one-week camp, the District Cub Scout six-a-side football competition and sports day, and attended the Pack 21 times during his illness.

While in hospital, he worked hard towards completing his Silver Arrow.

Andrew was awarded the Cornwell Scout Badge in recognition of his courage under extreme difficulties.

As you can see, courage shows in many different ways. There are lots more like these courageous Cub Scouts we have mentioned here – all doing their utmost to be good Cubs and to enjoy their Cubbing to the full. This determination to enjoy all that Scouting has to offer despite handicap and to put what they have learned in the Pack to good use in emergency situations, shows that being a Cub Scout is the best and those who are part of it can be considered as some of the best!

Express to adventure

by Hazel Addis

Illustrated by Edgar Hodges

Neil always felt rather sick on railway journeys. Now that he was travelling alone for the first time it seemed worse, because there was no-one to say "Are you feeling all right, Neil?" And he would answer, "Of *course* I'm all right," until he almost believed it himself.

He was going on holiday to his uncle in Devon and that meant a long time on the train.

Originally, he wasn't going on his own but then, just before they were due to leave, Dad was rushed into hospital with appendicitis and there was no way Mum was going on holiday after that! But Neil was nearly ten and a half and he was a Cub Scout – indeed, he would be going up to the Scouts in a matter of weeks – and anyway, the guard had agreed to keep an eye on him on his regular trips through the train and Uncle David would be on the platform at the other end to meet him so, slightly reluctantly, he had agreed to go on his own.

So now Neil was on the train and it smelt like old blankets and he was starting to feel a bit sick. He didn't want to read or eat, and after half an hour he knew he wasn't going to enjoy himself at all. The only other people in his carriage were a woman and a nasty little girl who seemed to be called 'Lovey'. The woman kept looking at Neil as though she knew he was going to be sick, and Lovey kept sucking sticky sweets.

After a while everything began to look rather green to Neil and the wall and the ceiling of the carriage seemed to be closing in on him, so that it was difficult to breathe. He screwed up his eyes for a moment and wished that the brakes would go on suddenly and that the train would stop.

And it did!

The brakes came on with a jerk and the whole train shuddered. Then it lurched on again and everyone was flung forwards and backwards and then sideways as the carriage reeled over. Neil grabbed at something and found, to his surprise, that it was the luggage rack which was lying in his lap. Everything seemed to be very unreal, just like a dream. There was a frightful noise going on, too: a crashing, banging, screaming and grinding, which just couldn't be real. Suddenly, the whole world turned upside-down.

Then there was silence.

Neil opened his eyes to find that he was still gripping the luggage rack – so it couldn't have been a dream. But he wasn't in a proper railway carriage anymore, he seemed to be lying on top of a junk heap. Most of it was scrap metal and bits of wood and odd things like suitcases and a window blind and a woman's shoe, and the whole place was full of dust and broken glass.

Neil lay still for a moment, trying to understand.

"Has the train crashed?" he asked. But no-one answered.

He let go of the rack and struggled to sit upright. At least he supposed it was upright. There was a window overhead where the roof should have been and, beyond it, another sort of scrap heap and, beyond that, a chink of blue sky.

Somehow this was very cheering and Neil looked up at it and announced: "The train **has** crashed!" He started to wriggle up towards the light, though there wasn't much space to move and now and then a loose bit of something gave way under his feet.

"Careful," said a voice, a very thin voice, which coughed and added: "there's broken glass everywhere."

Neil peered down into a dark corner of the rubble and saw the pale face of the woman, Lovey's mother, lying under a tangle of bits and pieces but with her head and shoulders clear.

"Are you all right?" he asked, slithering down carefully beside her.

"I think so," she said, "but there's something pinning my legs, so I can't move. But it's Susie – I must get to Susie!" She coughed and called, "It's all right, Lovey! I'm here!"

Neil could hear the child crying, somewhere out of sight. "She must be all right," he said, "to make all that noise!"

"Could you find her?"

Neil looked round helplessly and realised there were openings and gaps here and there, and dark tunnels more like a rabbit warren than a train.

The crying was coming from the other end of a rabbit hole and Neil started to squeeze into it. There was just enough space and, for once, he was glad that he was small for his age. But it was dark and dusty, and bits of splintered wood caught at his clothes. It could be rather frightening if one stopped to think about it. But Neil didn't stop. He went on squeezing and twisting until he found Susie, who was caught up in something by the belt of her coat.

"Oh, shut up," said Neil, as he wriggled up beside her. He tugged at her coat until the belt gave way, and she was free to grab him with both sticky hands. "Come on," he said, "and I'll take you to Mummy, but only if you promise to stop that noise!"

She hung onto him, only whimpering a little as they made their way through the bits and pieces. Somewhere there was the sound of hammering and, far away, voices shouting. But it was the voice calling "Lovey! **Lovey!**" that mattered and guided them back to where the woman lay.

"Careful of the glass!" she warned again, and Neil grabbed the child by the hair to hold her back.

He found a handkerchief in his pocket and flicked away the splinters of glass, so that Susie could crouch close to her mother. It was a red and white spotted handkerchief which Mum had given while she was telling him how everything would be all right and what fun he was going to have.

It helped him to say to Susie's Mum: "It's going to be all right, you know. People are looking for us."

"Could you shout or something?"

Neil tried to shout but his voice echoed around the junk heap and didn't seem to go much further. "You stay here," he said, "and I'll see if I can climb out."

There was that chink of blue sky.

If you have ever tried to climb a tree with broken branches and ivy and brambles growing all over it, you'll have some idea of what it was like for Neil trying to reach that chink of blue sky, except that the ivy was twisted steel and the brambles were splintered wood. But he did reach the top, only to find that it was much too small a chink to get through. He could just get his arm through the crack, but in his hand was the red and white spotted handkerchief and he held it high and waved it as much as he could.

It seemed a long time before he heard a shout from outside. It was a man's voice shouting: "Look, Joe! There's someone over here!" Then a hand grasped Neil's and a voice – oh, such a reassuring voice – said, "Are you all right?"

"Of *course* I'm all right," said Neil, and realised that he wasn't even feeling sick any more. "But there's a woman and a little girl a long way down inside all this mess."

"Hold on," said the man. "We'll get you out first."

"No, I'd better go back and wait with them," said Neil. "The mother's got her legs stuck and the kid's frightened."

So he took a big breath of lovely, fresh blue-sky air and started to wriggle back to tell the woman that everything was going to be all right.

It was three hours before they managed to release the woman, who had broken her leg. They hoisted her carefully up through the gap they had made. Then Neil pushed Susie up to them and climbed out after her.

Suddenly, everything seemed real again. Neil saw that it was only *their* coach which had been squashed almost flat in the collision. Several other coaches were derailed and one had reared up on end like a frightened horse, but the other passengers had been able to get out comparatively easily.

There were cranes and fire engines and men with cutting-torches and wonderful looking implements. Neil was just beginning to realise how exciting it all was, when he was bundled into an ambulance with Susie and her mother on a stretcher.

"She's not really my mother," Neil explained, although she smiled at him as though she was.

"Then we'd better have your name and address, son," said a policeman. "Your Mum will want to know where you are."

So Neil told him, and added, "And if you talk to Mum, tell her that I'm all right and I *am* having a *lot* of fun!"

St. David
(Wales)
March 1

March 1 is St. David's Day when many Welsh people will be seen wearing a daffodil or a leek.

David is the national saint of Wales and was born in the year 500. He was destined to become an important churchman and became the Primate of Wales, which is similar to an archbishop in England. David was hard-working and founded many monasteries.

Many legends have grown up around the Saint. One describes how fresh water would spring up at places where David prayed and that he had the power to miraculously heal the blind, lame and sick. On another occasion, he attended an assembly of bishops where anybody was free to speak. When David began to speak the ground rose up beneath him so that everybody could see and hear him.

One of the Welsh national emblems is the daffodil (David's flower) and, in Wales, they believe that if you are the first to find a daffodil in bloom then you will have more gold than silver for a year.

Another emblem is the leek. One of the stories behind the wearing of leeks tells how, after David's death, the King of Wales was preparing to fight Saxon invaders. On the eve of St. David's Day, he was informed that the Saxons were disguising themselves as Welshmen. The King decided that all true Welshmen should wear a leek, found nearby, to identify themselves. They were victorious in battle and, from that day on, to celebrate victory, every Welshman wore a leek on March 1.

You can learn about the other United Kingdom Patron Saints on pages 33, 48 and 63.

Action Stations — 1

Fun, games and activities from Norman Garnett and David Easton

Challenge

Everyone likes a challenge. Here are a few for you. Some of them are a bit daft. Some are quite serious. Some you can do on your own. Some are challenges that you can issue to the other Members of your Cub Scout Pack.

1. Have a competition to see who in your Pack can produce the biggest potato crisp.

2. Try eating a meal using chopsticks. If you do not have any at home, you can get some from your local Chinese restaurant. I am sure they will give you a set – providing the whole Pack don't go in and ask at the same time.

3. Write the alphabet on one side of a match. It can be done if you use a fine ball-point pen. Start off by practising on paper. Measure the length of a match on paper and write on that until you get very good at writing very small.

4. Light a fire on a 50-pence piece, and keep it going for five minutes. This is not easy, but I know that you can do it. It takes a lot of preparation. Challenge your Dad to see if he can do it. Then borrow his 50-pence piece!

5. Challenge the rest of your family to a jam doughnut eating contest. You each have a sticky, jammy doughnut. You have to eat the whole of the doughnut without licking your lips. It is nearly impossible. You can play the challenge in two ways – either you have to drop out as soon as you lick your lips; or score one point every time you have a lick. If you do it this way, the person with the lowest score wins.

6. Try writing or painting with the brush held between your toes. Lots of people have to do it this way because they do not have any arms or hands.

7. Challenge another Six to a Seven Welly Race.
   All six of you have to fit into seven wellies (big ones) like this . . .

.... HOLD ON TIGHT WHEN PUTTING ON THE LAST BOOT...

8. Send a Christmas Card or an Easter Card to someone who has been specially nice to you during the last year.

9. Make an edible zoo out of liquorice allsorts, jellies and other small sweets.

10. Be nice to your brother (or sister) for a whole day.

Useless

I heard one Cub Scout say of another, "Oh he never gets anything right. He is useless."

Have you ever felt like that about someone? Is there someone in your Pack or your class at school who you would want to dismiss as useless?

I hope not. Nothing can really be described as useless, and certainly no human being should be considered in that way. Some of us may be a bit dim, and we all have our own funny ways, but none of us is useless! You have to learn to find out everyone's good points and to make the best you can of them.

Here is a good way to remember this lesson. Think of a clock. You can take all the insides out of a clock so that it has nothing to make it go and nothing to make it tick. You would then think that as a clock it was 'useless'. But not so. Even though it had no works inside it, the clock would still tell the right time twice every day. And twice a day it would only be one minute fast; or one minute slow. Not useless at all!

Drop me a line

This is not an invitation to write to me.

I just want to show you how to make a line on a piece of paper disappear, without rubbing it out or covering it up.

Take a piece of paper or card, and draw on it 11 vertical lines. They should be exactly the same distance apart, and they should all end the same distance from each edge of the paper. It is worth taking a bit of trouble to measure them correctly, and it would be a good idea to do it in pencil very lightly to start with. Once you have checked that they are correct you can ink the lines in with a ball-point or felt-tipped pen.

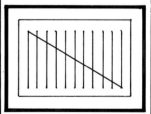

RULE THE LINES THE SAME DISTANCE FROM EACH EDGE

When you are happy that the lines are correctly drawn, take your ruler and draw another line from the top end of the first line, to the bottom end of the last line, as shown in the diagram below. You then cut along this line with a pair of scissors. Be careful!

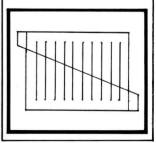

Place the two pieces back together again, but move the vertical lines along one space as shown in the third picture.

Now count the lines again. Instead of 11, there are only ten. One has disappeared!

What has really happened is that the extra line has been divided up into ten bits and one bit joined on to all the other ten lines.

If you do not believe me, you can check by measuring the length of each line.

Did you hear . . .?

Did you hear about the man who woke up one morning and found his bedroom full of aeroplanes?

When he went to bed the night before he had left his landing light on!

Did you hear about the showjumper who broke his nose jumping against the clock?

Did you hear about the undertaker who bought a new hearse?

People were dying to have a ride in it!

and finally

Did you hear about the man who went to the doctor and stood in the surgery all shivering and sneezing?

"Flu?" said the doctor.

"No, I came on the bus," he replied.

Eggs-actly

How to turn an egg into a submarine.

Try this experiment and baffle your friends.

You need two glass jars of the same size – big enough at the top to be able to put a hard-boiled egg inside.

Fill one of the jars with ordinary tap water, and the other one with strong salt water. If you get the jars ready beforehand, no one will be able to tell the difference because they will both look exactly the same.

If you drop the egg into the tap water, it will sink right to the bottom of the jar. If you drop one into the salt water, it will float near the top. This is because the salt water has a greater 'density' than tap water.

Those of you who can swim may have noticed when you are on your holidays that it is much easier to float in the sea than it is in your local swimming pool. That is because the sea is salt water.

But back to the eggs. If you pour both lots of water into a larger jar, you may very well find that you have a solution which has exactly the same density as the egg, and it will not know whether to sink or float. By adding extra water from each of your jars in turn, you will be able to make the egg rise and fall in the water like a submarine.

Keep experimenting, and see if you can get the egg to float half-way up the jar.

Ouch!

There was a young Cub Scout
 called Paul
Who narrowly missed a
 bad fall.
He broke seven teeth
And the jawbone beneath,
Three ribs and a leg,
 but that's all!

IN TOUCH WITH THE WORLD

To help you keep in touch with the world, British Telecom has thousands of miles of undersea cables that fan out from the shores of the UK towards Europe and North America. A series of communication satellites, orbiting thousands of kilometres up in space, carry not only millions of phone calls each year to more than 200 countries, but also television pictures, data, text, graphics and an ever increasing range of other services.

All customers in the UK can dial their own telephone calls to more than 180 countries worldwide and in so doing reach 93 per cent of the world's telephones – that's about 600 *million*!

But what exactly happens when you pick up the phone and dial the number of your pen-pal abroad? Let's follow one such call . . .

Tom lives in Brentwood, a town just to the east of London. He wants to call his pen-pal who lives in a town called Domasi in Malawi. To reach his pen-pal in Malawi, Tom must dial 010 265 531 123.

Here's how the number breaks down:

010 international code	**531** local exchange in Malawi
265 country code	**123** individual phone number

An engineer works at one of the familiar green cabinets which are dotted around our streets.

A well-known London landmark – the Telecom Tower, clearing-house of many of the United Kingdom's overseas calls.

Calls to Malawi (and, of course, those to many other destinations, too) are passed along microwave towers to Madley Earth Station, situated near the town of Hereford.

Here's what happens when Tom makes his call:

When Tom first picks up the phone, he automatically gets a dial tone from the local exchange. This means that the call has travelled from his house to a green cabinet in the street and on to the nearest local exchange.

– 0 –

This first digit indicates that the call is not local and will be going out of the local exchange. At the local exchange, the call goes into a switching bank and into what's called a trunk network.

– 1 –

The second digit indicates that the call is en route for the London exchange. (Note that **01** is the code for London.)

– 0 –

The third digit indicates where the call is to go in London. The **0** directs the call to the International Exchange, or International Switching Centre. There are five of these

centres in London called Keybridge, Kelvin, Mondial, Thames A and Thames B. A call to Malawi goes through Mondial.

– 265 –

This group of numbers is the international code for Malawi. These numbers also indicate the way in which the call is to be routed – by satellite or cable. Calls to Malawi are usually sent via satellite from Madley Earth Station.

When a call is sent by satellite, the signal is combined with others going the same way, sent on to the Telecom Tower – in London – and sent by a chain of microwave towers positioned every 50km to Madley Earth Station.

Once at the earth station, the signal is processed by a complex set of equipment. It is 'electronically parcelled' up with a host of other signals going the same way, labelled and identified as being destined for Malawi.

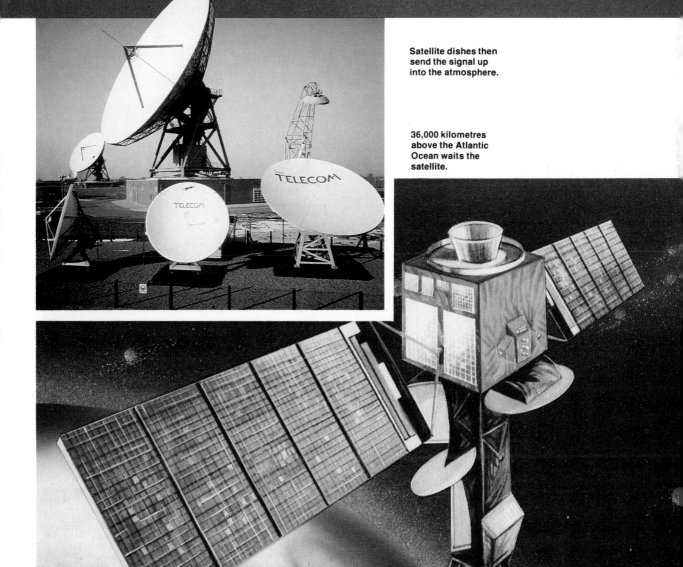

Satellite dishes then send the signal up into the atmosphere.

36,000 kilometres above the Atlantic Ocean waits the satellite.

The parcels are then amplified and converted to a higher frequency and, after further processing, travel on to the large dish aerials. The aerial is pointed at one of several possible satellites above the Atlantic – and the 'parcels' of radio signals are sent up to the satellites at the speed of light, 298,000 kilometres per second. It takes but a fraction of a second to travel the 36,000km to the satellite, where the frequency is changed and the 'parcels' are retransmitted in a beam directed towards the earth station serving Malawi. The 'parcels' are then unwrapped and the signal continues its journey through the exchanges in Malawi and to the person dialled.

The reverse process takes place in Malawi. The call is picked up by Soche Earth Station in Malawi and sent to the Balaka Microwave Tower. Then the call is distributed inland via microwave to the main exchange at Balaka.

– 531 –

The numbers **531** indicate that the call is intended for the town of Domasi. The call goes through the main exchange at Balaka to the local exchange in Blantyre.

– 123 –

The **123** is the individual's number. The call goes from the local exchange to Tom's pen-pal.

The sound of the telephone ringing in Malawi makes the return journey to Tom, at home in Brentwood, in less than a second.

It's a fact . . .

The world's first scheduled telephone call via the communication satellite Telstar, was made on July 26, 1962. Leslie Madden from Rugeley, Staffordshire, spoke to Howard Knowlton in Western Springs, Illinois, USA, for seven minutes. Leslie Madden said at the time that their historic phone call would be 'an inspiring portent of the future' – and this has certainly come to pass. Incidentally, the call came to a sudden end when the Overseas Operator interrupted – to clear the line for the next caller!

The 1990 Cub Scout Annual extends its thanks to British Telecom for its help in the production of this feature.

Balaka Microwave Tower receives the call.

Malawi's Nichev Microwave Station continues the chain of communication.

A familiar cabinet routes the call on the last stage of its journey – last, that is, until the signal reaches the telephone and the ringing tone bounces back along the same route while the bell summons someone to answer it.

Cliff Brown's Music Puzzle Page

FIND THE MUSICAL INSTRUMENTS. A GROUP OF KEEN SCOUTERS MANAGED TO GET A COMPLETE BAND TOGETHER BUT, JUST BEFORE THEIR FIRST PERFORMANCE SOMEONE HID ALL THEIR INSTRUMENTS. CAN YOU HELP FIND THEM?

WHO IS THE COMPOSER AND WHAT DID HE WRITE? FILL IN THE ACROSS CLUES TO READ HIS NAME DOWN THE SHADED SQUARES. THEN COMPLETE THE LOWER BOXES FOR HIS FAMOUS TUNE.

A MUSICAL JUMBLE. JIM IS WONDERING WHAT INSTRUMENT HE COULD PLAY TO GET HIS MUSICIAN PROFICIENCY BADGE. HOW MANY CAN YOU SORT OUT IN HIS JUMBLED THOUGHTS?

MEET THE CHIEFS

Lord Robert Baden-Powell

The Lord Somers

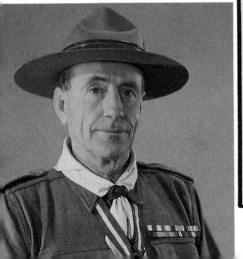

The Lord Rowallan

Lord Robert Baden-Powell of Gilwell, OM, GCMG, GCVO, KCB Chief Scout of the World 1908–41

Robert Stephenson Smyth Baden-Powell was born in Paddington, London on February 22, 1857. He was the eighth of ten children born and his father, the Reverend Baden-Powell, was a Professor at Oxford University.

Robert Baden-Powell would have won a place in the history books even if he had not founded the Scout Movement. He had a brilliant career as a soldier and became a national hero for his defence of Mafeking in 1899. So brilliant was that defence that he became a Major-General at the age of only 43. It was during this 217-day siege that his book *Aids to Scouting* was published and gained a wide readership back in England – particularly among youth leaders and teachers.

In 1912 he married Olave Soames, who later became the World Chief Guide. Baden-Powell was acclaimed Chief Scout of the World at the first International Scout Jamboree at Olympia, in London. In 1929 he was created a peer and took the title of Lord Baden-Powell of Gilwell. He died in 1941 and is buried in Nyeri, Kenya.

The Lord Somers, KCMG, DSO, MC Chief Scout 1941–44

Arthur Herbert Tennyson Somers-Cocks, 6th Baron Somers, was born at Freshwater, Isle of Wight on March 20, 1887. Educated at Mulgrave Castle, Charterhouse and New College, Oxford, he joined the 1st Life Guards but cut short his army career to farm in Canada. With the outbreak of World War I he returned home to rejoin his regiment. He retired from the army in 1924 – two years after having become involved in Scouting.

In 1926 Lord Somers was appointed Governor of Victoria, Australia and became Chief Scout of that State. He led 8,000 British Scouts to the World Jamboree in Holland in 1937. The following winter he helped to put Scouting on a firm financial footing by launching a national appeal. He worked tirelessly for the Movement and when war broke out in 1939 he gave an immediate lead in support of National Service. He recommended that Scouts wore their uniform and wore his in the House of Lords.

He was elected Chief Scout on January 29, 1941 and travelled long distances to attend rallies and conferences, despite his failing health. He died on July 14, 1944.

The Lord Rowallan, KT, KBE, MC, TD, LLD, DL Chief Scout 1945–59

Born in London on December 19, 1895, Thomas Godfrey Polson Corbett was educated at Eton. World War I broke out when he was 18 and he went straight from school into the army, serving at Gallipoli, and in Egypt and Palestine. He won the Military Cross in France but a severe leg wound put paid to what might have been a brilliant military career. In 1933 he succeeded to his father's peerage.

He joined the Scout Movement in 1922 as a District Commissioner. His involvement with the Movement progressed until, in 1944, he became the Scottish Headquarters Commissioner for the Training of Leaders. Just before the outbreak of World War II, Lord Rowallan was asked to raise a new Battalion of the Royal Scots Fusiliers which he trained along Scout lines. After Dunkirk he was given command of a Young Soldiers' Battalion and later he was made responsible for training potential officers.

In 1945 he became Chief Scout of the Commonwealth and Empire. After he left in 1951 he was appointed Governor of Tasmania and retired in 1963. He died in November 1977 at Kilmarnock.

The Lord Maclean, KT, GCVO, KBE Chief Scout 1959–71

Born Charles Hector Fitzroy Maclean on May 5, 1916, the fourth Chief Scout was educated at Canford School in Dorset. With a regular commission in the Scots Guards he served in the Guards Armoured Division and the 6th Guards Tank Brigade and he saw service during World War II in France, Belgium, Holland and Germany. He left the army in 1947 with the rank of Major.

He was a Cub Scout in London in 1924 and after becoming Chief Scout in 1959 he visited some 50 countries to promote the Movement. He was also appointed Chief Scout of the Commonwealth. He succeeded to the title of 11th Baronet of Duart and Morven in 1936 and as the 27th Chief of the Clan Maclean, he lives at the ancient stronghold of the Clan on the Isle of Mull. He is married and has a son and a daughter.

He instituted the Advanced Party Report in 1966 which shaped the Movement for the future. In 1971 he was given a life peerage by the Queen. That same year he was appointed Lord Chamberlain and resigned as Chief Scout. He stayed as Chief Scout of the Commonwealth until 1975. In July 1981 he organised the wedding of HRH Prince Charles and the Lady Diana Spencer.

The Lord Maclean

Sir William Gladstone, Bt, DL, MA Chief Scout 1972–82

Sir (Erskine) William Gladstone, great-grandson of the former Prime Minister, William Ewart Gladstone, was born on October 29, 1925. Educated at Eton, he joined the Scouts while at the school. He saw war service in the Royal Navy which he joined in 1943 and, on leaving the service, he gained a degree at Oxford before entering the teaching profession. He became Headmaster of Lancing College in 1961.

Sir William is married to Rosamund Anne Hambro and they have two sons and a daughter. In 1968, Sir William succeeded his father as 7th Baronet. The family home is at Hawarden Castle, Deeside, Clwyd, in Wales. He also owns an estate in Kincardineshire, Scotland.

As Chief Scout he took a special interest in the development of Scouting in deprived areas, particularly in the inner cities. In 1979 he was elected Chairman of the World Scout Committee.

Sir William Gladstone

Major-General Michael J. H. Walsh, CB, DSO, DL Chief Scout 1982–88

Major-General Michael Walsh was born in Harrogate, Yorkshire in 1927 and attended Clifton House School where he was a member of the school Scout Troop. He has the distinction of being the only Chief Scout who was a boy Member in both Cub Scouts and Scouts and he became a King's Scout. He also holds the Gold Cords which, in their time, were the Movement's highest training award for proficiency and achievement.

He has had a distinguished army career, rising from the ranks to become a Major-General. He retired from the army in 1981 after holding the position of Director of Army Training. He married Angela Beswick from Sheffield and they have two daughters. An active communicant of the Church of England, he has wide ranging interests in the arts, music and sports. He is a qualified Royal Yachting Association Coastal Skipper, holds a private Air Pilot's licence and is a qualified parachutist.

Michael J. H. Walsh

Garth Morrison, DL Chief Scout from 1988

(William) Garth Morrison became Chief Scout as recently as 1988 at the comparatively young age of 45. By profession a farmer, Garth had previously served in the Royal Navy. He attended Britannia Royal Naval College in Dartmouth and while there was awarded the Queen's Telescope in 1962, one of six awarded that year. Still in the Navy he then went to Pembroke College, Cambridge and gained a Bachelor of Arts degree and a year later gained Dartmouth's top award, the Queen's Sword.

Among many other notable achievements the present Chief Scout is a Member of the Guard of Honour at the Palace of Holyroodhouse and has been Her Majesty The Queen's Deputy Lieutenant in East Lothian since 1984.

Before becoming Chief Scout of the United Kingdom and Dependent Territories, Garth Morrison was Chief Commissioner of Scotland and has held several other Scouting appointments.

Garth Morrison

STUNNING STUNTS

by Dave Griffiths

If you have been a Cub Scout for some time now, you have probably been away on a Cub Camp or Pack Holiday. While there you might even have gone to a camp fire when everyone sang songs and perhaps some Cub Scouts or Scouts performed a stunt or two. These, just in case you don't know, are very short and usually funny plays, which often last just a couple of minutes. Anyone can perform these stunts and, below, are a few that you could learn to start you off. Before that, however, here are a few tips that could help you.

When you are planning a stunt, remember, it is important that nobody gets upset by what you perform so your stunt shouldn't be hurtful and you should never make fun of people with a disability or those who follow a religion different from your own. Likewise, using water or, say, an egg to make one person wet or messy may be funny at the time, but it's not much fun for that person having to sit through the rest of the camp fire in wet or sticky clothes.

The secret of good comedy is 'timing'. This means making sure that your stunt is the right length – if you talk and act too quickly, the audience won't understand what is happening but if you are too slow the audience will get bored and start fidgeting. This means that you must practise first, to get it just right. Also, everyone involved needs to know exactly what they must say and do and precisely when they must say it and do it. You may need to use 'props' (clothes or other items) to help the story and these can be improvised and it is often funnier if they are exaggerated – instead of using a teaspoon to administer medicine, for instance, use the largest serving spoon you can find!

Remember, prepare your stunts well, learn your lines and actions and speak in a loud, clear voice.

After all this, you're bound to be a huge success so 'break a leg' (that's the actors' way of wishing each other good luck).

Water, Water!

4 boys. 3 cups. 1 comb.

Boy crawls into camp fire circle. (If his clothes can look dusty, so much the better.) He has obviously been crawling through the desert for days. All he can say is: **"Water! Water!"** He continues to crawl around the circle.

A Cub rushes in with a mug. **"I've got some coffee."** The first boy shakes his head and repeats his plea – **"Water! Water!"**

A second Cub rushes in with a mug. **"I've got some cocoa."** The first boy shakes his head and continues crawling around the circle, groaning **"Water! Water!"**

Eventually the last Cub enters. He rushes up to the lad with a mug in his hand. **"Here you are – water!"** Slowly, the boy pulls a comb from his back pocket, dips it in the water and begins to comb his hair!

Life in the desert

5 boys. One of whom acts as an introducer. The four boys line up next to one another. One has a cup of water in his hand. The rest will need to have a mouthful of water stored in their mouth.

Introducer: "**Life in the desert is tough – any water has to go a long, long way.**"

The first Cub takes a swig of water from the cup. He gargles with it in his mouth, then leans over to the next Cub and pretends to squirt it into his ear (in fact he swallows it).

The second Cub, having already got a mouthful of water then gargles with it – swishes it around in his mouth and leans to the next Cub, and pretends to squirt it into his ear.

The third Cub does the same, and leans to the fourth Cub and pretends to squirt the water into his ear.

As soon as the fourth Cub is supposed to have received the water he swills the water around in his mouth and spits it out on the ground, exclaiming: "**Yeuch! I do hate lukewarm water.**"

A cup of water

2 boys. A cup and a supply of water.

A boy stands in the camp fire circle. A Cub Scout rushes up to him and says: "**Can I have a cup of water, please?**"

The boy walks out of the camp fire circle (slowly) and returns with a cup full of water. He gives it to the Cub Scout who rushes out with it.

A few moments later, the Cub returns with the empty cup. "**Could I have another cup of water, please?**"

The boy takes the cup, walks out of the circle and returns with a cup full of water. The Cub says thank-you and rushes out of the circle. The lad remaining starts to look puzzled (perhaps shrugging his shoulders).

This continues a few more times, until eventually the Cub Scout returns for a final time. "**Could I have another cup of water, please?**"

The boy takes the cup and says: "**Boy – you must be very thirsty!**"

The Cub replies: "**Oh I'm not thirsty – your tent is on fire!**"

They both rush out of the circle.

Lone Ranger

5 boys. One Cub dressed as the Lone Ranger, one Cub dressed as Tonto, three Cubs dressed as Indian medicine men. A pair of large Wellington boots, a cup of water and some flour.

Lone Ranger and Tonto enter circle.

Tonto says: "**Kimosabi – him lose his voice. I seek Medicine man to make him better.**"

1st Medicine man enters. He is carrying a pair of Wellington boots.

Tonto says: "**Kimosabi – him lost his voice.**"

1st Medicine man: "**I have solution – we try this pair of magic boots.**"

He puts the boots on the Lone Ranger. Lone Ranger opens and shuts mouth several times, as if he is trying to speak.

Tonto says: "**Magic boots no good. Kimosabi still lost voice.**"

1st Medicine man leaves.

2nd Medicine man enters. He carries the cup of water.

Tonto says: "**Kimosabi – him lost his voice.**"

2nd Medicine man: "**Magic potion made by tribal witch doctor – this will bring back Lone Ranger's lost voice.**"

Lone Ranger drinks the water, then opens and shuts his mouth several times without any result.

Tonto says: "**Magic potion no good. Kimosabi still lost voice.**"

2nd Medicine man leaves.

3rd Medicine man enters. He has some flour in his hand.

Tonto says: "**Kimosabi – him lost his voice.**"

3rd Medicine man: "**This magic powder will make Lone Ranger talk again.**" Medicine man takes a little flour and pats it under the Lone Ranger's armpits. Then he sprinkles some over the Lone Ranger's shoes.

The Lone Ranger speaks: "**I have my voice back – I can talk again.**"

Tonto says: "**How you know this powder would work?**"

3rd Medicine man says: "**Easy! This is TALK-UM POWDER!**"

The Dixie

4 boys. A long pair of socks, a large dixie and a ladle will be required. The socks and ladle must be placed in the dixie before the start.

First boy walks into the camp fire circle, places a large dixie near to the fire and walks off. (Nothing is said – the audience will be waiting to see what is going to happen next!)

A second boy walks into the circle. He picks the ladle up out of the dixie and pretends to taste the contents. He pretends to savour the taste (like a wine connoisseur) then swallows and exclaims loudly: "**Needs more salt**". He pretends to shake an imaginary pot of salt into the dixie before leaving the circle.

A third boy enters. He repeats the actions of the second Cub Scout – tasting, savouring and swallowing. He then says loudly: "**Not enough seasoning**". He rubs his fingers together over the dixie (like crumbling a meat stock cube). He then leaves the circle.

A fourth boy enters. Repeats the actions and exclaims: "**Too sharp! I'll add some sugar**". He pretends to do so, then leaves.

Finally, the first lad comes back. He takes the dixie from near the fire and places it on the ground. He looks into the dixie and then at the audience. "**Yes, yes. I think so!**" He bends down and pulls out his socks – "**They should be clean by now!**"

TODAY'S THE DAY

illustrated by
John Shackell

6th January 1918 Captain J. Hedley fell out of his plane at 1,500 feet, during a steep dive while trying to evade enemy fighters. The dive was so steep that the pilot was literally plucked from his seat. His co-pilot levelled off a few hundred feet lower and discovered that his incredibly lucky pilot had been swept backwards by the slipstream and was sitting on the tailplane!

1st February 1811 The wind-swept Bell Rock Lighthouse was first lit. The 115 ft edifice, 24 miles east of Dundee, had taken over four years to build and every stone in its construction had been dragged from Arbroath by one horse.

20th February 1917 The Englishman with the longest surname died of pneumonia in the trenches during World War I. His full name was Major Leone Sextus Denys Oswolf Fraudati Tollemache-Tollemache de Orellana Plantagenet Tollemache Tollemache. His men called him 'Sir'!

14th January 1878 The first private telephone call was made by Queen Victoria. Her Majesty found it 'rather faint', but she and her friends had great fun singing and reciting poems into it. In fact they could just as well have shouted out of the window – the recipient was in a cottage on the estate, just a few yards away!

16th February 1955 Soviet surveyors surprised the world when they announced that they had overlooked something in Siberia. It was a 24,664 ft high mountain they hadn't noticed before!

MOUNTAIN? WHAT MOUNTAIN?

25th March 1738 An unholy accident was narrowly avoided when Will Summers and his colleague were hanged for house-breaking. The hangman was drunk and thinking there were three to be dispatched, was only 'with much difficulty' restrained from stringing up the parson!

16th April 1902 Eccentric French publisher Aurelian Scholl died. His strangest venture was to publish *La Naïade* (The Water Nymph), a newspaper printed on rubber so that it could be read while bathing!

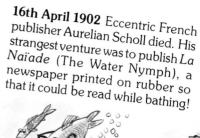

4th March 1849 David Rice Atchison took the helm of the United States for a whole day. President Polk's term of office had expired but his successor, Zachary Taylor, refused to be sworn in on a Sunday. As President of the Senate, Mr Atchison automatically became President in the interim. He confessed afterwards that he had slept all day — his entire term of office!

25th May 1935 Record wrecking black athlete Jesse Owens broke the world records for the 100 yards, 220 yards, 220 yards low hurdles and the long jump — all in 45 minutes!

4th May 1780 The first ever Derby was run on Epsom Downs, Surrey. Inaugurated by the 12th Earl of Derby and Sir Charles Bunbury, there was some disagreement over what the race should be called. It was finally resolved when the two founders tossed a coin. Had the Earl not won, this world famous horse race would now have been called 'The Bunbury'. Sir Charles did receive some consolation, though, as his horse won the first race.

8th April 1845 One of the Duke of Wellington's homing pigeons established a record that has never been reliably broken. It was released from a ship off the coast of West Africa. If it travelled as the crow flies it would have covered some 5,500 miles but it probably detoured around the desert and so flew nearer to 7,000 miles. The bird was found a mile from home in London — stone dead from exhaustion!

4th June 1974 A friendly turtle saved the life of Mrs Candelaria Villanueva when the ship she was on caught fire and sank. The giant sea turtle supported her in the water for over 36 hours until she was rescued. Throughout her ordeal she was kept awake by another turtle — a tiny one who climbed up her back and gently nipped her ear every time she felt drowsy!

21st June 1890 Unlucky matador Luis Freg was born. His was the dubious honour of being gored more times than any other bullfighter. He got the point 57 times and was given the Last Rites five times, but always came back for more. Eventually he retired from the ring — and drowned two years later.

27

3rd July 1839 Mathematical wizard Vito Mangiamele was examined by the French Academy of Sciences. The learned gentlemen were amazed at his remarkable ability to solve complicated mathematical problems at lightning speed. He gave the cube root of 3,796,416 in just 30 seconds. Vito was 11 at the time!

10th August 1975 Lightning struck an unfortunate umpire during a cricket match at Berwick-on-Tweed. Although he recovered, he found great difficulty in walking – the flash had welded solid the metal joint in his leg!

1st September 1271 The longest papal conclave ended when Theoboldi Visconti became Pope Gregory X. The College of Cardinals had spent 31 months in the Vatican without coming to a decision. Finally, they were put on bread and water and, quite literally, the roof was taken from over their heads. Agreement was reached shortly afterwards!

9th July 1787 Mad Dr Elliot attempted a double murder in a London street. He fired a brace of pistols at a courting couple at point blank range. Somehow he missed them both, although the lady's dress was badly singed. At his trial his lawyer cited that as no bullets could be found no one could prove that the guns had been loaded. Incredibly, Elliot was found 'Not Guilty'!

13th August 1930 A historic drive reached its halfway stage when Charles Creighton and James Hargis arrived in Los Angeles after chugging 3,340 miles from New York. Twenty-three days later, they made it back again. The incredible thing was not the distance, but that they did it each way without stopping the engine – and entirely in reverse!

13th October AD 54 The Emperor Claudius was murdered by his wife, Agrippina. First she fed him a dish of poisoned mushrooms: he collapsed but his servants thought he was drunk and carted him off to bed. Determined Agrippina then got the physician to tickle the back of his throat with a feather dipped in poison. This didn't work either so in the end they smothered him with a cushion!

25th September 1825 A cormorant's stomach revealed a strange secret. A hunter watched the bird, flying low over the water, snatch up a fish and retire to the bank to eat it. The hunter shot the bird and when opening its 'maw' later found a gold brooch valued at £10 inside!

18th October 1961 A picture went on show at an exhibition in New York and it attracted vast crowds. But none of the 116,000 people who looked at it in the next 46 days noticed that it had been hung upside-down!

8th December 1670 Henry Jenkins died in Yorkshire at the reputed age of 169 years. He could not read or write but could recount convincing details of the Battle of Flodden Field 157 years earlier and also of life during the reign of Henry VIII. There were five other centenarians in his village who could not remember him as anything else but 'a very old man'.

28th December 1869 Chewing-gum was patented by an American dentist. He saw it as an excellent way to exercise the jaws, stimulate the gums and scour the teeth. Famous for its sticking qualities it was used to help the dirigible R-34 across the Atlantic. When a leak was discovered in the water-jacket of one of the engines and no glue or putty on board could stop it, chewing gum was handed round to the crew, chewed rapidly and shoved in the hole. It worked and the R-34 completed its journey safely.

16th November 1841 An application was submitted for a US patent for the first cork-filled life-jacket. Though widely used it didn't gain Federal approval for 36 years until, with the sinking of the *SS San Francisco*, this ignored invention proved its worth by saving 287 lives.

15th November 1699 The 'English Samson', William Joyce, appeared before King William III. As a demonstration of his strength he lifted a solid piece of lead, weighing over a ton; then, roped to 'an extraordinary strong horse' he kept it at a standstill even when it was whipped. The day before, however, he had surpassed even these feats by uprooting a tree at Hampstead. Its trunk was one and a half yards (metres) round!

These curious happenings have been reproduced with the kind permission of W. H. Allen & Co Ltd from their publication *Today's The Day!* by Jeremy Beadle.

A VERY SPECIAL

One in ten guide dogs are German Shepherds.

It is now quite a common sight to see a blind person with guide dog walking along the street. But have you ever wondered how the dogs lead their owners around the neighbourhood without getting them lost, while at the same time guiding them around obstacles or dangers, up and down stairs, through bustling crowds and even on and off buses or trains?

Guide dogs are obviously highly trained animals. Indeed they have to go through a tremendous amount of training and, each year, The Guide Dogs For The Blind Association trains up to 120 dogs at each of their seven training centres. Most of these come from their own Breeding Centre, sited near Warwick, and, right from the day the pups are born, the Centre's staff monitor each one. It is important that they discover, as early as possible, which of the youngsters will 'make the grade' – most of them do, but not all. The qualities they are looking for

are that the dog must be fit and healthy, it must have the correct temperament and it must show a willingness to please.

Until they are six weeks old, the puppies remain with their mother but then they are taken away and put into the care of families, known as 'Puppy-walkers'. These are specially selected volunteers who take a dog into their home for 10 to 12 months. During this time they teach it to be clean, respond to simple obedience commands (such as 'sit', 'stay', 'come' and so on) and generally let the dogs get used to home life, people and children as well as the hustle and bustle of a family's existence. Once a month, they are visited by a 'Puppy-walker Supervisor' who keeps a check on the dog's progress.

When their time is up, the young dogs go back to the Training Centre to start their primary training.

All puppies are reared at The Association's own breeding centre.

FRIEND

by Thomas Morgan

There are now over 4,000 working guide dogs.

The tests are tough!

Learning to walk in the middle of the pavement, not going around corners until they are asked and mastering 'formal' commands (like 'forward', 'back', 'left' and 'right') are the next stages in the dog's learning progress and each animal must meet the very high standards laid down by the Guide Dogs Association. When it passes these tests (and it must pass *all* of them) the dog then goes on to the next phase in its training – learning to sit at the kerb and then cross the road in a straight line when given the command to do so.

A few weeks into this stage of training the dogs are introduced to wearing a harness – essential for guiding their blind person in the future. A brown harness indicates that the dog is in training, while a white harness means the dog is with a blind person. The harness is fitted with reflectors and is strapped to the animal around its back and tummy and across its chest. The young dogs have to learn that when they are wearing the harness it means that they are 'working' and they must, therefore, concentrate exclusively on leading their owner along safely.

And get tougher still

During the next five months, the training intensifies as, in the care of a specially qualified instructor, they are taught to watch and listen for traffic and only to cross the road when it is safe for them and their blindfolded instructor to do so. Special obstacle courses prepare the dogs for other hazards that might occur (like, for instance, roadworks or dustbins left in the way) and also get them used to assessing the size and height of gaps so that they can decide if there is enough room for both them and their blindfolded instructor to pass through safely.

The last few weeks of advanced training are spent getting the dog ready for its new owner. Great care is taken when matching dogs with blind owners as it is very important that they suit each other perfectly – a more elderly or retiring person would, for instance, need a quieter dog whilst a more outgoing person may perhaps require a more boisterous dog.

A guide dog can give a blind person independence and a chance to lead a normal life.

Dogs are carefully trained to fit in with the lifestyle of their new owners.

organisation and relies on the generosity of the public for its funds.

The cost of training to these very high standards is obviously not cheap, in fact it costs £1000 to sponsor the cost of breeding the dog and training the dog and blind person. A £2000 donation also covers the cost of food and veterinary bills. The sum of £250 sponsors the cost of rearing a puppy.

You could help. A good deal of fund raising is done by collecting and saving aluminium foil, ring-pulls off the top of cans and used postage stamps.

You could do this, too, as a Pack or as a Group, getting the Beavers, Scouts and Venture Scouts to help. Ask Akela to contact your nearest branch of The Guide Dogs For The Blind Association for one of their Information Packs. These give details of the work of the Association and include ideas and suggestions on fund raising. Your Pack may like to make a visit to a centre, to see the kennels where the dogs stay during their training. There is a guided tour as well as a film show and a talk by a guide dog owner.

But remember . . .

When a guide dog is working (when it is in its white harness) it needs to concentrate fully on its job – any distraction, for instance if you talk to the dog or pat it, could lead to an accident. Therefore, just let them get on with their work. But when they are not working, they are just like any other dog and will enjoy 'normal' doggy activities.

Likewise, don't feed them tit-bits or sweets. Many dogs have to have a special diet so that they keep their weight at the right level.

Puppy-walkers ensure that the young dogs become accustomed to all types of public transport.

When the Association is satisfied the dog is completely safe and sure, blind people from a waiting list are invited to stay at the Training Centre for four weeks and in this time dogs and humans are taught to work safely and confidently together. Mutual confidence is essential and an instructor is always on hand to help iron-out any problems that arise.

Help and advice, in the first few weeks after their return home, is given through regular visits from a Guide Dog Instructor and, through these, the dog will quickly get to know local routes, shops and even its blind owner's place of work.

On average a guide dog will have a working life of 8 to 9 years, after which they are put into well-earned 'retirement'. Often they will be kept as a pet by the blind person and their family but if this is not possible then a good home will be found for them by the Association.

Costs

The Guide Dogs For The Blind Association is a charitable

The *1990 Cub Scout Annual* thanks The Guide Dogs For The Blind Association for their help in compiling this feature and for supplying the photographs.

32

Patron Saints of the United Kingdom

by Hazel Chewter

illustrated by
Colin Smale

St. Patrick
(Ireland)
March 17

St. Patrick is the Patron Saint of Ireland and his day is celebrated on March 17 each year.

Patrick was born in England at the end of the fourth century and at the age of 16, he was kidnapped by pirates, taken to Ireland and sold into slavery. He worked as a herdsman and after six years he managed to escape and return to his family. Not long afterwards, Patrick had a dream in which he heard the Irish people calling him back to them. He was unwilling to return uneducated so, after training as a priest, Patrick returned to Ireland to teach his beliefs. In his teachings, Patrick used the shamrock to explain the three-fold nature of the Trinity and this was quickly adopted as the symbol of Ireland.

The most popular legend about St. Patrick tells how he banished snakes from Ireland. When he had first gone to Ireland, the people were troubled by snakes. As the Saint had walked through the country, all the snakes fled into the lakes and only emerged in very remote places. Patrick decided that, before he died, he had to banish all snakes. One farmer was being particularly troubled by a large snake living in a lake bordering his land. At night it would come out and steal his sheep and cattle. Patrick ordered the snake to leave the country, but all the time the snake was in the lake it felt safe and refused to go. Then, Patrick realised that he would have to change the water in every lake in Ireland so he knelt down by the water and started to pray. The snake suddenly felt the water changing. It stung and burned him so much that he rose to the top, thrashing his large tail, and then raced off to the sea where the water was cooler and where he would be safe from Patrick. This happened throughout the country and Patrick continued to pray until the last snakes had fled to the sea. From that day to this, not a single snake has been found in Ireland.

You can learn about the other United Kingdom Patron Saints on pages 15, 48 and 63.

Action Stations – 2

Fun, games and activities from Norman Garnett and David Easton

Percy

Here is a good game for two players. It doesn't last long and you will want to play another game as soon as you have finished the first.

You need a piece of paper and ten matches or cocktail sticks.

On the piece of paper, draw seven lines next to each other. They should be about the same length as the matches or sticks, and they should be slightly less than that apart.

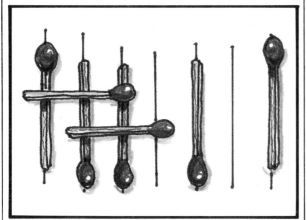

Each player has five matches. Sit on opposite sides of the paper with the lines pointing to the players. Toss up for who goes first. Each player, in turn, places one match on the paper. They are placed on the lines. If you are using matches you can make sure that the score is kept accurately by each player placing the matches with the coloured end nearest to himself.

When there are two matches side-by-side, a player can choose to play his next match across the other two. Only one match can be placed on any set of two.

Scoring is as follows: Every time you play a match on a line, you score one; and every time you play one sideways across two others, you score two.

You will see when you try the game, that you have to try to force your opponent into letting you score twos, and that your third, fourth and fifth matches are the most important.

Pip, squeak and Wilfred

Of all the games my Cub Scouts have played, the ones they have liked best have always been the daft ones.

Here is a particularly daft one which you might like to try.

You will need:
1. *A pip.* An orange pip or a grapefruit pip. Anything smaller is just a bit too small to pick up easily.
2. *A squeak.* Any baby's squeaky toy will do. The louder the squeak, the better.
3. *And Wilfred.* This is where the real fun begins. 'Wilfred' consists of a bucket containing any horrible gooey mess. It can be made out of anything that is messy, colourful, sticky and generally 'gungy'. Try a good mixture of wallpaper paste, flour, water and poster paint – you really can put anything in it so long as it is messy!

It also makes sense to have a lot of newspapers to cover the floor, or a large plastic sheet to go under the bucket.

The game itself is very easy, and you probably already play it in some other form.

All the Pack sit in a large circle. They number off in threes, 1-2-3 1-2-3 1-2-3 etc.

The Leader calls out a number and adds either 'pip', 'squeak', or 'Wilfred'.

As soon as your number is called out you jump to your feet and race round the outside of the circle until you get back to your own place and then into the middle. If your Leader called 'pip', you simply pick up the pip before anyone else grabs it. If the call was 'squeak', you grab the toy and give it a good squeeze. If you are lucky enough to get the call 'Wilfred', you simply have to plunge your hand into the gooey mess in the bucket. Great!

I strongly suggest that you only play this game when there are washing facilities available. It is definitely not a game for a Christmas party at home – unless you live in a barn!

Peter

Teacher: "Peter, say a sentence beginning with I."
Peter: "I is . . ."
Teacher (interrupting): "No, Peter. You must say I am . . ."
Peter: "Sorry, Miss. I am the ninth letter of the alphabet!"

Peter: "Doctor, will my measles have gone by next week?"
Doctor: "I cannot say. I never make rash promises."

Peter: "Every day my dog and I go for a tramp in the woods."
Paul: "Does the dog enjoy it?"
Peter: "He sure does. But the tramp is getting a bit fed up!"

Geography teacher: "Peter, where is Felixstowe?"
Peter: "On the end of Felix's foot, Miss!"

It's a gift

Everyone likes to receive a gift.

Or do they?

We certainly all like to receive birthday or Christmas gifts, but it is surprising how often we are suspicious of other gifts. Almost every day I receive letters through the post from firms and businesses who have bought my address from someone else, offering to give me free gifts. This all sounds very well, but the gifts never turn out to be quite 'free'. "If you will spend your money with us," they say, "we will give you a free diary, pen, record or whatever . . ." It usually means that I have to agree to buy something else to qualify for my 'free' gift – and that hardly seems like 'free' to me.

A man who I used to work with would never take any sort of gift off anyone – he always thought that you must want something in return. We always used to buy cakes for each other on our birthdays but he spoiled it all by refusing to join in. I tried to persuade him that he didn't have to buy them himself, and that I was quite happy to buy him one without expecting anything in return. He made such an issue of it that in the end we all stopped buying cakes, and the office was a much sadder place. We were all quite glad when he went to work somewhere else. What a sad sort of man he was.

I once heard of another man who stood in the street and tried to give away pound coins to passers-by. Nobody would take them. They were all suspicious – they thought that there was a catch in it.

The giving and receiving of gifts should make everyone happy. There is one gift that you can try to give away every day.

It is a smile.

Funnily enough, it is a very hard gift to get rid of, because as soon as you give a smile to someone, they almost always give you one back. Try it and see!

See how long it takes you to get rid of a smile.

If you give it to someone and they give you one back, then you have not succeeded in giving it away, and you have to try with someone else.

I once tried this little game in Manchester on a wet Monday morning. As I walked across the city to go to work, I tried to give my smile away. Even though Manchester on a wet Monday morning is not the 'smilingest' place on earth, it was not easy. One or two people looked at me as if I was crackers, but most people gave me one back. And the harder I tried to give it away, the harder it became. The more I did it, the better I became – perhaps we all need to practise, just like playing the piano.

Go on. Give it a go.

Spread a little happiness.

Fund raising

At some time or other during your time in the Cub Scout Pack, you will be called upon to raise some money for something.

It may be because your Headquarters needs a new roof, or it may be for the Blue Peter Appeal, or Children In Need.

Fund raising ideas are not easy to come by, especially those that raise large amounts. However, many of the old ideas which raise small amounts at jumble sales and Christmas fairs can be good fun to run. If you are asked to help at such an event, try the Malteser Bashing Contest.

You will need an old, strong table which will take a bit of bashing about. A fairly long cardboard tube, a box of Maltesers, and a mallet are the only other things you need.

The tube should be about 50cm long. Prop it up at one end of the table.

The contestants hold the mallet at the side of the table.

You roll a Malteser down the tube and they have to try to smash it with the mallet when it shoots out of the bottom. They are only allowed one bash! Do not have too long a table otherwise they will be able to wait until it slows down.

Charge them a penny a hit, or 5p for six goes.

Try not to eat too many of the Maltesers as you are playing!

MALTESER IN HERE

HENRY

I'VE BEEN IN AND OUT OF HOT WATER SO MUCH I FEEL LIKE A TEABAG..

Sun's rays

SUN

Earth's atmosphere

EARTH

WATER CYCLE

The sun's energy evaporates the water in the seas, lakes and rivers, which later falls as rain or snow.

(A) Water collects in the seas, lakes and rivers.

(B) Water evaporates and condensation forms clouds of minute water droplets. Some of these water droplets grow in size until they are sufficiently large to fall as rain.

(C) Over hills and mountains rainfall is greatly increased. Where the temperature is below freezing snow falls.

(D) Snow collects on mountains and forms a GLACIER (E).

(F) All water in the hills runs down into LAKES (G), STREAMS (H) and RIVERS (I) and so eventually rejoins the sea.

SUN

The sun is the central star of the solar system. It is a giant mass of burning gas situated approximately 93 million miles (149 million km.) from earth. All light, warmth and energy on earth come from the sun. Only a fraction of the sun's energy reaches us as the power of the rays is broken down by the earth's atmosphere.

SUN RECORDER

A sunshine recorder focuses the sun's rays onto a thick card and scorches a record of the sunshine.

WIND

Wind is the movement of air caused by difference in pressure. The air tends to move from higher to lower pressure but because of the earth's rotation the wind spirals anti-clockwise in towards the centre of a depression, and clockwise outwards from an anti-cyclone. As wind blows from different points of the compass it brings air of varying temperatures and weather types.

Cool & showery with sunny spells.

Cold & showery. Very cold in winter.

Mild. Warm in summer. Moist & humid. Often cloudy with rain or drizzle.

Cold in winter. Hot in summer. Dry.

BEAUFORT SCALE In 1806 Sir Francis Beaufort made a scale to measure the speed of wind.

BEAUFORT NUMBER	WIND	WIND SPEED M.P.H.	EFFECT OF WIND OVER LAND
0	Calm	1	Smoke rises vertically.
1	Light air	1-3	Smoke drifts.
2	Light breeze	4-7	Leaves rustle, wind felt on face.
3	Gentle breeze	8-12	Leaves move, light flag is extended.
4	Moderate breeze	13-18	Dust and loose paper blow about. Small branches move.
5	Fresh breeze	19-24	Small trees sway a little.
6	Strong breeze	25-31	Large branches sway, wires whistle.
7	Moderate gale	32-38	Whole trees sway, hard to walk against the wind.
8	Fresh gale	39-46	Twigs break off trees, very hard to walk into wind.
9	Strong gale	47-54	Chimney pots and slates blown off. Large branches down.
10	Whole gale	55-63	Trees uprooted, serious damage to buildings.
11	Storm	64-72	Very rare inland, causes widespread damage.
12	Hurricane	72 +	Disastrous results.

ANEMOMETER

An anemometer measures wind speed and wind direction.

introduction to WEATHER

Reproduced by kind permission of Premiums & Print Ltd, Leicester, from the Kellogg's Wallchart.

CLOUDS

Water vapour is always present in the atmosphere and it condenses into water droplets in several ways. You see these visible water droplets in the form of clouds. In the short term clouds provide one of the best indicators we have to changes in the weather. At sea or in the mountains the approach of clouds can be observed from a great distance and can give a good weather guide over the next few hours to the amateur weather forecaster. The important thing to remember about weather forecasting is that it is a combination of factors that tell you about the weather—clouds, pressure, wind direction, temperature, etc.

CIRRUS (Mare's tails)

CIRRO-CUMULUS (Mackerel sky)

CUMULUS (Fair weather clouds)

CUMULO-NIMBUS (Thunder clouds)

An introduction to
THE WEATHER

ATMOSPHERE

The earth is enclosed in a layer of air, called the atmosphere, which extends upwards for approximately 700 kilometres. This atmosphere, which is a mixture of gases, gets thinner, or less dense, as height increases. It is the movement of air within the atmosphere which brings different weather conditions.

THINGS IN AND ABOVE THE ATMOSPHERE

Weather satellite 1,000 km.

Aurora Borealis 70-1,000 km.

Heatshield of space ship burns at 200 km.

Meteoroids burn out at 200 km.

Weather balloon 25 km.

Jet plane 12 km.

Cirrus cloud 6,000-18,000 m.

Mount Everest 8,900 m.

AIR PRESSURE

Above every square foot of the earth's surface there is a column of air, the weight of which presses down and is called air pressure. The air pressure changes from day to day and is a very important element in weather forecasting. Aneroid barometers measure the change in air pressure and help to indicate the kind of weather which may be expected. Weather balloons are also used to measure air pressure.

WEATHER BALLOONS

Weather balloons are filled with hydrogen gas roughly equivalent to the air pressure at ground level. As the balloon rises the air pressure lessens causing the balloon to grow bigger and eventually burst. Weather balloons carry a small automatic radio transmitter called a radiosonde which is fitted to instruments measuring temperature, air pressure and humidity. As the balloon rises the radiosonde records and transmits the measurements at different heights above the earth. The balloon is also tracked on radar and from this the weatherman can work out the speed and direction of the winds at various heights. When the balloon bursts the radiosonde falls back to earth on a small parachute. The readings it contains help the weathermen to forecast the forthcoming weather.

SNOW AND ICE

Snow is formed in a similar way to rain except that the temperature is below freezing point and the water vapour forms ice crystals instead of raindrops. The crystals grow within the cloud, cluster together and form snowflakes which fall to the earth.

SNOW CRYSTALS

These are always six-pointed stars, but no two snowflakes will be exactly the same.

DEW AND FROST

Dew and frost both occur on still clear nights. When the sun sets, the earth cools rapidly and so does the layer of air close to it. Some of the water vapour in this condenses to form a dew on the ground, or if it is below freezing point, a frost.

MIST AND FOG

Mist, like a cloud, is made up of tiny droplets of water, but whilst clouds are formed by the cooling of rising air, mist is formed by contact with cold air close to the ground. Fog is a thick mist and is formed in exactly the same way. At sea, mist or fog is caused by warm air blowing over the cooler water of the sea.

°F	°C
140	60
105	40
95	35
85	30
75	25
70	20
60	15
50	10
40	5
32	0

THERMOMETER

The temperature of the air is measured by a thermometer in degrees, either on the Centigrade or Fahrenheit scale. The freezing point of water is 0°C or 32°F. Temperatures are always recorded in the shade, out of the direct rays of the sun.

ANEROID BAROMETER

The easiest way for ordinary people to forecast the weather is to consult an aneroid barometer and note if the pressure is rising or falling. Rising pressure is a sign of weather improving and falling pressure means bad weather. The most important component in the barometer is the vacuum box. A fall or rise in the air pressure causes the box to contract or expand. This expansion and contraction is very slight so a system of levers magnifies the movement, which is finally displayed by a needle moving round the dial.

(A) Vacuum Box
(B) Base Plate
(C) Frame
(D) Steel Spring
(E) Lever
(F) Magnifying mechanism

(G) Chain connecting magnifying mechanism with Spindle (H)
(I) Return Spring
(J) Indicator Needle
(K) Dial

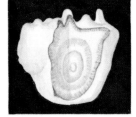

HAILSTONE

A hailstone is a frozen water drop. This one has four coats of ice which indicates it has travelled to the top of the cloud four times.

THUNDERSTORMS

Thunderstorms can and do occur at any time of the year and in any part of the country. You can watch the sky and see how thunderstorms build up. First little fluffy cumulus clouds form on a clear day. They grow bigger and taller until their tops spread out into an anvil shape where ice is forming and rain falls from the cloud. The ice tries to fall but each time strong currents of air carry it back to the top of the cloud. This action of rising and falling causes electric charges, with the top of the cloud building up a strong positive charge and the bottom a strong negative charge. Eventually the build-up of electricity becomes so strong that the current flashes and this is what we see as LIGHTNING. Lightning can occur inside a cloud or between a cloud and a positive charge on the earth. The lightning flash heats the air to white heat so that it expands very rapidly to produce the sound wave we hear as THUNDER.

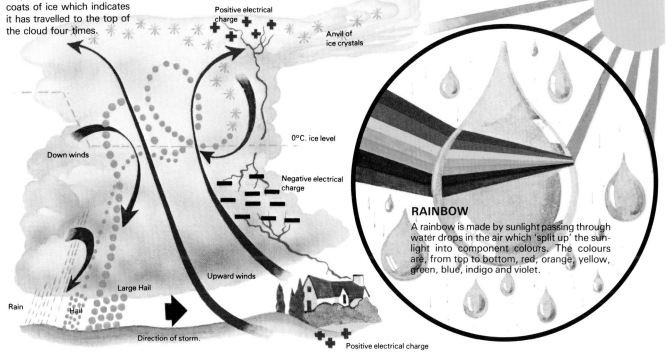

Positive electrical charge

Anvil of ice crystals

0°C. ice level

Negative electrical charge

Down winds

Large Hail

Rain

Hail

Upward winds

Direction of storm.

Positive electrical charge

RAINBOW

A rainbow is made by sunlight passing through water drops in the air which 'split up' the sunlight into component colours. The colours are, from top to bottom, red, orange, yellow, green, blue, indigo and violet.

MODERN FORECASTING

The modern weather service gets reports from many places and people; weather satellites, aircraft, weather balloons and observations made over land and sea from most of the Northern Hemisphere. This information is analysed by computers and the weatherman then works out the forthcoming weather. Weather reports and forecasts are given out by radio, television and the press and this information is vital to seamen, farmers, sportsmen and many other people who need to know what the weather is going to do.

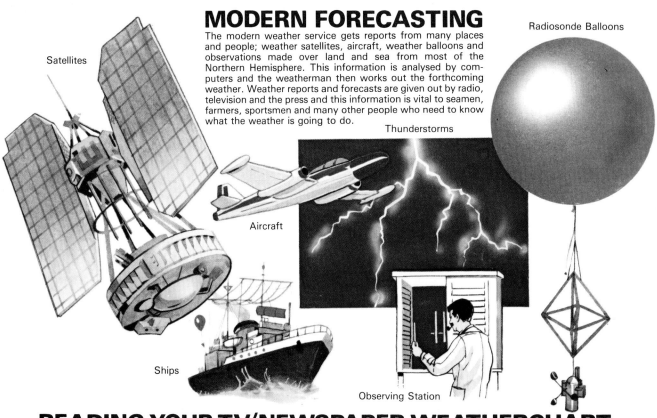

Satellites

Radiosonde Balloons

Thunderstorms

Aircraft

Ships

Observing Station

READING YOUR TV/NEWSPAPER WEATHERCHART

The illustrations shown here are typical of weather charts seen on television and in newspapers. Weatherchart No. 1 shows a 'low' or a depression; weatherchart No. 2 shows a 'high' or anticyclone over the same area. Barometer pressures are shown on weathercharts in millibars. Isobars are lines drawn on the charts through places having the same pressure, and are drawn for intervals of 4 millibars (see charts). Wind arrows are not normally shown on charts, they have been put on these examples to indicate that winds blow clockwise around areas of high pressure and anticlockwise around areas of low pressure in the Northern Hemisphere. If the isobars are close together it indicates high winds and if far apart it indicates light winds. Fronts are boundaries between masses of air of different origin and are indicated as follows: ▬●●●▬ warm front; ▬▲▲▲▬ cold front. The symbols are placed on the side of the line towards which the front is expected to move.

WEATHERCHART NO. 1
DEPRESSION (PRESSURE LOW AT CENTRE)

The weather pattern is moving eastwards over the British Isles. The barometric pressure will fall quickly as the depression approaches, and rise behind it. Depressions usually bring disturbed weather, strong winds and rain, with perhaps snow in winter. Frequently most of the rain, or snow, is associated with fronts and depression centres. Cooler, brighter and sometimes showery weather follows after the cold front has moved away.

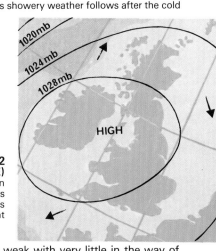

WEATHERCHART NO. 2
ANTICYCLONE (PRESSURE HIGH AT CENTRE)

Frequently a slow moving weather pattern. Usually more settled and bright, but in winter, clear skies and light winds can mean frost or fog. If high pressure persists over northern Europe in winter, then this can mean a spell of very cold east winds for Britain. In summer however, high pressure over the British Isles or the continent usually brings fine warm weather.

These two examples can only give a general idea of this very complicated subject. For example, depressions often change their shape and speed of movement quite rapidly. They can intensify to give gales and stormy weather or become weak with very little in the way of weather and wind. Which way they will develop and move is one of the problems that forecasters have to resolve.

Compiled with the kind assistance of the Meteorological Office, Bracknell, Berks.

Cliff Brown's Explorers Puzzle Page

SIGN POST MIX-UP.

THIS LAD IS A TRIFLE BEWILDERED—THE SIGNWRITER STARTED WRITING THE TOWNS BUT ENDED THEM WITH ANOTHER TOWN. CAN YOU SORT THEM OUT?

LONCHESTER
BLACKSTONE
BRISTWYTH
LANHAMPTON
NOTTINGSTOKE
GLASWICH
MANDON
BASINGHAM
SOUTHCASTER
NORGO
ABERYSTOL
FOLKEPOOL

THE ROCK CLIMBERS. STUDY THE BOTTOM PICTURE CAREFULLY THEN LOOK AT THE DETAILS OF IT IN THE CIRCLES. SOME ARE TAKEN FROM THE PICTURE, OTHERS ARE FAKES—WHICH ARE WHICH?

TO GET YOUR EXPLORER BADGE, YOU MUST BE ABLE TO MAKE A FIRE. CAN YOU PUT THE FOUR-LETTER CLUES IN ORDER, SO THAT THERE IS ONE LETTER CHANGED EACH TIME TO END WITH FIRE?

FIRE

St.Tiggywinkles

Everyone knows that hedgehogs roll themselves into a ball when they feel in danger – presenting their enemy with a mass of spikes. While this is very effective against most other animals and, indeed, even against humans, it is no form of defence against that huge metallic beast that moves at incredible speeds – man's motor car! It is a sad fact that every year approximately 100,000 hedgehogs are run over and killed on our roads.

But our motor transport is not the only danger that threatens these harmless little creatures, for many more of them are killed accidentally by well-meaning humans feeding them the wrong foods – usually bread and milk (they much prefer a saucer of dog- or cat-food and a bowl of water).

Still more perish each year through eating plants and insects sprayed with chemical pest-control agents.

And every November 5 sees hundreds more literally roasted alive after they have inadvertently crept into the base of bonfires as they were being built, believing that here was somewhere warm, dry and safe to curl up in to hibernate for the winter.

So, as you can tell, life is no picnic for a hedgehog!

But the chances of them being hurt or injured do not end here – for there are times when hedgehogs can be a danger to themselves! Dozens of these timid little creatures injure themselves when they get trapped in plastic bean-netting or in the cotton (usually black) which gardeners stretch over newly-planted seeds to keep the birds off. Once caught in something of this sort, hedgehogs will fight!

They will twist and turn, getting themselves even more caught up until they end up nearly severing a leg or damaging their throats. Likewise, they will injure themselves in trying to get out of any sort of cage.

Help!

But help is at hand! For in the town of Aylesbury, in Buckinghamshire, is St. Tiggywinkles – the world's first hedgehog hospital unit. St. Tiggywinkles is in business purely for the benefit of injured hedgehogs.

Since the Centre was officially opened in August 1985 by actress Susan Hampshire, they have cared for hundreds of these spike-covered creatures and, on average, they have between 100 and 150 'in-patients' at any time.

The facilities they offer, while pretty basic in human terms, are positively palatial when seen from an injured hedgehog's point of view.

Obviously, there is no 'public' money available for a venture of this sort (hedgehogs are not covered under the National Health Service!) and they have no money of their own, so St. Tiggywinkles has to rely on donations of cash and equipment to keep going. Their first 'ward', for instance, was a smart timber shed which was donated by a local firm of gatemakers and their first incubator was provided by the British Petroleum Company (which would in a human hospital only be used by one baby at a time, easily holds up to eight premature baby hedgehogs!).

World-class expertise

The care and first aid that St. Tiggywinkles provides is excellent. Although in the early days much of the work was on a trial-and-error basis (because there was, literally, no one who *knew* how to tend for sick and injured hedgehogs) this is no longer the case. Over the years they have had to deal with all manner of ailments and injuries until now they are respected as world experts on the care of sick hedgehogs – indeed, they are reckoned to be the animal equivalent of St. Bartholomew's Hospital – and they are consulted by vets throughout the hedgehog-inhabited world. (There are no hedgehogs in North or South America, in Australasia or the Polar regions.)

Well again

Nowadays the recovery rate is high and many of the nation's prickly little animals owe their lives to the care and attention they have received from the kind staff at St. Tiggywinkles. One of the main problems of taking any form of wild animal into human care is that it may grow to depend on it, in which case it would not survive very long back in its own environment. This is something which St. Tiggywinkles is very much aware of and, at the very earliest opportunity but *only* when the creature is fully fit and well, it is released into the Buckinghamshire countryside – hopefully, never to return to St. Tiggywinkles Hedgehog Hospital again!

You can help

If you would like to know more about how *you* can help these defenceless little creatures you can contact St. Tiggywinkles at: 1 Pemberton Close, AYLESBURY, Buckinghamshire HP21 7NY. They will be pleased to send you a free fact-sheet and details of how you can adopt or support one of their hedgehogs together with advice and information about how to care for and look after one that might visit your garden.

No ambulances

But if you come across a sick or injured hedgehog in your garden, or by the roadside, how do you go about getting it to St. Tiggywinkles? Unfortunately, unlike when a human gets hurt, you can't just call an ambulance. But there are two ways of getting the hurt creature to assistance.

Firstly, you can take it to St. Tiggywinkles yourself. Many people, from all corners of the country, have done just this. They have placed the casualty *gently* into a small box lined with some old, clean rags (to keep the patient warm and comfortable) and then journeyed by public transport or car to Aylesbury.

The alternative method is to use the British Rail 'Hedgehog Express'. This service means that unwell or hurt hedgehogs, carefully packed, again in old, clean rags, but this time in a bucket, can be sent – for a fee of £10 – to Aylesbury overnight by BR's Red Star Service.

St. Tiggywinkles kindly provided the photographs that illustrate this feature.

43

SO YOU WANT TO BE A SCOUT NOW . . .

by Chris Atkinson

"Stop fidgeting about." Akela hissed the words out of the corner of her mouth. Well . . . it was all a bit embarrassing really. I had to stand there in front of everybody while Mr Davies, the Group Scout Leader, went on and on about what a great Sixer I had been. And how it was going to be just great in the Scout Troop, wasn't it? *It was*, wasn't it?

When I started my Link Badge I thought it would be a bit different in the Scouts, but at first they all made a fuss of me. Peter, he's the Patrol Leader of the Hawks, said that they were the best Patrol in the Troop and that it was terrific that I'd got my Gold Arrow. Peter's got a lot of badges, and so have the rest of the Patrol. I'm going to have to wear a new shirt with no badges, but Peter said we're going to do something which will get everybody in the Patrol a badge. Doing the Link Badge was fun and I went to the Scout Christmas camp for a whole day, we did some forestry work and then burnt our names onto pieces of wood with a hot wire.

"Stop day-dreaming," whispered Akela, giving me a nudge, "it's time to move." I took a deep breath and stepped forward.

Seems to me like that ceremony took place ages ago; I've been a Scout for two months now – that's eight Troop Meetings and one Troop hike. The hike was a laugh because it rained like mad just beforehand, and we came back with mud up to our ears – at least that's what my Mum said. I'm going to get a proper pair of boots like the

M. CLIFFORD

others in the Hawks because Mr Devenish, he's the Scout Leader and we call him Dev, says that we do lots of hikes when we're at camp. Some of the Scouts walk ever so fast so I walk with Darren Walsh who used to be in Green Six, he came up to the Troop last year. I wonder how Blue Six and Akela are managing without me.

We had this wide game the other evening. We all went up to the local camp site and then set up bases in the wood; we had to defend our flag and also try to capture another Patrol's flag. We had coloured wool on our arms, and if someone from another Patrol grabbed this then you had lost your life and had to go back to Dev for a new one. I got chosen for the raiding party and it was really great because we had to crawl silently through these bushes to get close to the other site. We got ever so close without being seen and then Peter jumped up and ran away making a lot of noise. This was our plan to distract the guards, and it worked. Two of us dived into the clearing, grabbed the flag and ran like mad back to our site. Or we would have done if another Patrol hadn't ambushed us on the way, and Darren trod on my fingers!

I've got a badge! It's the Swimmer Badge, and Dev's going to present it to me at next week's Meeting. Peter says that if I practise hard I could get into the Troop team for the District Swimming Gala. There's a course for the Fireman Badge starting soon, and you have to go along to the Fire Station in the evenings and learn all about fire precautions and fire fighting. Dev says that it's always a

M. D. SMITH

W. M. SMITH

popular course, but he'll put my name forward. Peter says that the badge the whole Patrol is going to get is called the Patrol Activity Award. We'll have to do everything together, and Peter says that we are going in for a cooking competition and that will get us the Award. I don't know if I'll be able to cook as well as the others.

Dev came round and saw my Mum and Dad last night and I can go to Summer Camp! We're going to the Lake District and it's going to be fantastic. Dad says he'll get me a proper rucsac and sleeping-bag from the Scout Shop. Dev says that I'll need to attend the Whitsun camp and a Patrol camp beforehand to get some experience – try and stop me! Anyhow I've been camping with the Cubs so I am experienced already; Dev says it's a bit different with the Scouts though.

It's more fun now that the evenings are lighter, we've started doing things outside the Troop room. This Friday we put up the Patrol tents and checked that the canvas was in good condition, and that we all had the right number of poles and pegs. We've got red rings on our tent poles and pegs, this is so that everyone can see that Hawks are the greatest! Last week we built a tower out of poles and with a platform for us to sit on. We were supposed to make a cup of tea up there, but I knocked over the milk and it went all over the grass so that was that. The rest of the Hawks said they'll let me live this time!

Whitsun camp was just great. Our site was by this backwater and we were able to use the canoes. Some of the Venture Scouts came along and they showed us how to do an Eskimo roll, one of them said that I was good enough to go for my Canoeist Badge. We had a super camp fire on the Saturday night and we did a stunt where we all had to pretend we were penguins. Afterwards we had our Patrol midnight feast in the tent, but nobody else knew because we were ever so quiet. You could see ever so many stars in the sky, and Peter showed me which was the Plough and how to find the pole-star. Our Cub Scouts came out to visit us on Sunday. Dev told us all to look after them and let them see what the Scouts did. We had to watch them all the time – they kept getting into everything and rushing around all over the place when I was trying to show them how I helped build our altar fire. Cub Scouts are really noisy you know!

I didn't go to Summer camp after all; I got measles instead. Dev and Peter came round to see me just before they went to camp; they said not to worry because there would be loads more camps. They didn't come right inside my bedroom though!

I was well again in time for the Cooking Competition, and we came second out of the whole District and got a special certificate each. Peter says that for all the work we've done the Patrol Leaders' Council has agreed that we have earned the Patrol Activity Award – great!

Dev says that Michael Porter from Red Six is going to start his Link Badge and will I be sure to welcome him and look friendly or something. I remember Michael Porter from when I was Blue Sixer, and Dev says that he's got his Gold Arrow though I can't think how. They must give them away these days. He's going to find it a bit different with us, I expect he reckons that he's top gun in the Cubs. He doesn't know yet that it's magic and that it all happens right here in the Scouts. But once we start to get him trained he'll be okay.

WILDLIFE IN CAMOUFLAGE

**written and illustrated
by Peter Harrison**

**Many animals have evolved ingenious
ways of disguising themselves to enable
them to hide from their enemies or to
prey on others.
These pages show you some . . .**

THE PTARMIGAN changes its plumage
according to the season of the year.

THE HERMIT CRAB carries its home
on its back and hides away when it
senses there's danger about.

THE GRASS SNAKE sometimes
pretends to be dead, which is
one of the ways it protects
itself from its enemies.

THE STOAT in its winter
and its summer coat.

Some harmless insects imitate unpleasant
species like the WASP to make other creatures
imagine they are more harmful than they really are.

HOVER
FLY

WASP
BEETLE

HORNET
MOTH

WASP

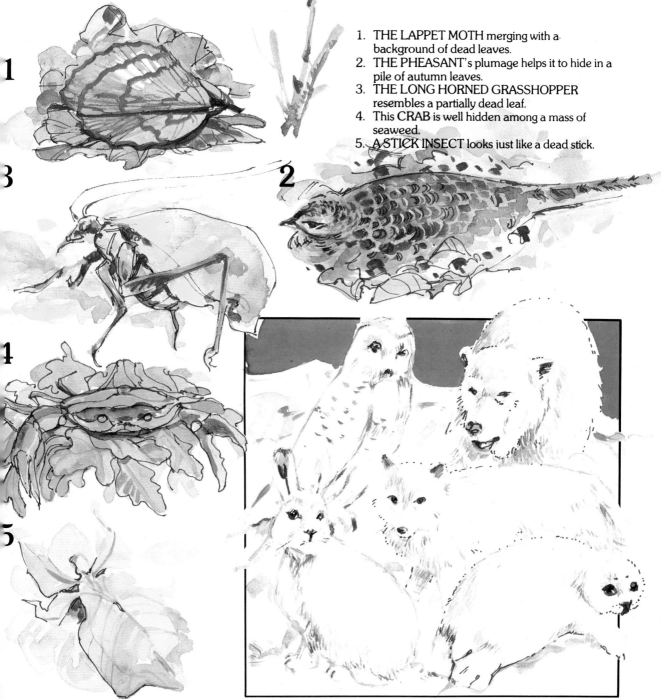

1

3

2

1. THE LAPPET MOTH merging with a background of dead leaves.
2. THE PHEASANT's plumage helps it to hide in a pile of autumn leaves.
3. THE LONG HORNED GRASSHOPPER resembles a partially dead leaf.
4. This CRAB is well hidden among a mass of seaweed.
5. A STICK INSECT looks just like a dead stick.

4

5

THE SNOWSHOE HARE, SNOWY OWL, POLAR BEAR, ARCTIC FOX and SEAL PUP all live in Arctic conditions, merging into their white habitat.

THE CABBAGE MOTH is dull coloured and well camouflaged.

Most FROGS and TOADS live on the ground and are coloured in shades of green and brown, helping them to hide in the mud and vegetation in which they live.

Patron Saints of the United Kingdom
by Hazel Chewter

illustrated by
Colin Smale

St. George
(England)
April 23

St. George is the Patron Saint of England (and also of Scouting), but it is not possible to say with certainty just who he was and what he did. He was probably born around the third century and is thought to have been Greek.

The most famous legend about St. George is the one which tells of his adventure with a dragon. The dragon lived in a large pond on the edge of a small town, and not only did it have a vicious tail but it also had poisonous breath.

For a long time the villagers had been trying to destroy the dragon but all efforts had failed. They even sacrificed sheep to it, until all the sheep were gone and then the villagers put all their own names into a hat and had to pick out the name — one each evening — of the dragon's next victim.

One day, it was the Princess' name that was picked and she went to offer herself to the dragon. Just as it emerged, St. George came along, saw what was happening, pulled a scarf over his face, charged into the attack and thrust his spear into the dragon's throat. The Princess then led the dying dragon back to town where St. George chopped its head off.

St. George was not known in England until the Crusades, when he is said to have appeared on several occasions to lead the English to victory. George was adopted as England's Patron Saint and his banner, an upright red cross on a white background, became the flag of England and the red rose, the most prolific flower of England, became the country's emblem which many people can be seen wearing on St. George's Day, April 23.

You can learn about the other United Kingdom Patron Saints on pages 15, 33 and 63.

TIN CANS and VACUUM CLEANERS

An empty cat-food tin, an empty coffee tin and a vacuum cleaner! Not quite what you'd expect to use for a series of highly successful scientific experiments, but these were the things Christopher Cockerell used to build his first working model of a hovercraft.

Mr. Cockerell, who was later knighted for his important pioneering work in the invention of the hovercraft was not, as you might expect, an aircraft engineer but an electronics engineer. In 1950, after some 15 years working on electronic research, he

bought a small boatyard on the Norfolk Broads. He had always been interested in boats and wanted to learn all he could about the theory of boat design. He noticed that when a boat was moving at high speed, its hull tended to lift out of the water and the faster the boat travelled the more the hull would lift above the surface. He decided that if he could lift the hull of a boat completely out of the water he would remove the friction, or 'drag', between the water and the hull. A series of experiments eventually led to the tin can model and, in 1956, his first working model was demonstrated.

An AP1-88 hovercraft operating near Vancouver in Canada.

An SRN-1 with Christopher Cockerell on board, landing at Dover after the first cross-Channel flight on July 25, 1959, the 50th anniversary of Louis Bleriot's first cross-Channel aeroplane flight.

The 'secret' list

The invention was shown to the British Armed Forces and immediately was put onto the 'secret' list. Work continued until the full potential of the invention was realised. Within a year, hovercraft were off the 'secret' list and, on July 25, 1959, the first full-scale hovercraft, the SRN-1, made its debut as it crossed the English Channel. SRN-1 measured some 30 feet (9.5 metres) long, was about 24 feet (7.25 metres) wide and was powered by a single 450 horsepower engine.

Several companies became interested in this new form of transport, most of the early research and development being carried out by Britain's leading aircraft and shipbuilding companies.

Justified optimism

A well-known encyclopaedia, published in 1961, stated: 'It is possible that large hovercraft, perhaps weighing many tons, may one day be in service.' An optimistic forecast, coming only two years after

These AP1-88's operate a regular service to the Isle of Wight and carry the Royal Mail across (note the Mail van) as well as passengers.

the first public demonstration – but was it justified? On August 1, 1969, the SRN-4 hovercraft *Mountbatten,* weighing 165 tons and carrying 250 passengers and 30 cars, entered the Channel service between Dover and Boulogne. In its first 12 months of service it proved to be 95 per cent reliable and carried one million passengers and one hundred thousand cars!

Versatile

Since those early days, the hovercraft has proved to be one of the most versatile forms of transport in the world. It can travel equally well over land or sea and can move from one to the other and back again with no need for any sort of modification.

Its versatility means that it can also be used in swamp land where a tracked or wheeled vehicle

An SRN-6 Mark 5 in service with the Interservices Hovercraft Unit.

would sink but it can still carry the same, or, in some cases, an even greater payload. Hoverpads, which are simply non-passenger carrying adaptations of the hovercraft, are used in many heavy construction industries to move massive loads over unsuitable roads or soft ground. Loads as large as 700 tons have been moved in this way.

Another bonus of the hovercraft is that, due to its lack of friction against either land or water, it needs very little power to move it along.

Remarkably swift development

It is remarkable that the invention of the hovercraft was developed much faster than almost any other form of transport. For example, the first demonstration of an automobile took place in 1885 but it was not in service until 16 years later. The first aircraft was demonstrated in 1903 and it was 16 years before there was one in passenger service. The helicopter, which is often thought of as being a fairly recent invention, was, in fact, first demonstrated in 1907 but it did not come into service until 1950 – a whole 43 years later!

So the hovercraft, which, as early as 1962, saw the SRN-2, a 27-ton craft carrying 50 passengers at 139kph in a regular service, was a very swift developer indeed! For just 3 years had passed between its first demonstration and its appearance in regular passenger service. Since then, the hovercraft has become part of our everyday lives and many of you will have already travelled on one of these remarkable craft, perhaps going to or coming home from holiday. But if you haven't already done so then this is something you should try to put right as early as possible – it is an experience not to be missed and you will never forget the thrill of speeding across the land or water on a cushion of air.

The photographs for this feature were kindly supplied by Hoverspeed Ltd., British Hovercraft Corporation (a Westland Aerospace Company) and Mr. John Hendy.

The Royal Navy also makes use of hovercraft. This one is on mine detection and disposal trials.

Speedy answers to calls for help are provided by Canada's Coastguard in one of their SRN-6 Mark 1's.

Travel to and from France is made easy and quick with the regular service provided by Hoverspeed craft which operate from the Kent coast.

No room in the stables

Hazel Addis

ILLUSTRATED BY IVAN HISSEY

This is the story of a donkey called Neddy, who lived nearly two thousand years ago, but he really looked just the same as any donkey today.

He lived with a nice family of sheep and goats, dogs and cats, chickens and two cows, both called Moochy. It wasn't a farm but an inn, which we would call a pub nowadays. People like the inn-keeper always kept that sort of animal-family – looking after them in exchange for eggs from the hens, wool from the sheep and milk from the cows, while the dogs and cats protected them all from rats and robbers. Neddy's job was transport, as the Boss often rode him to market.

They were all very happy, except perhaps for the Moochies, who always managed to find something to grumble about.

People were always coming and going at the inn – mostly tired travellers who wanted a meal or a bed for the night – which meant that their animals had to share the stable with inn-animals.

Then, one night, something extraordinary happened . . .

All day the little inn at Bethlehem had been extra busy, with people arriving from all over the place – tired, hungry strangers mostly arguing about some tax they had to pay. Of course, the inn-animals didn't know what a tax was, but they rather enjoyed all the excitement, listening to the stories the strange animals had to tell and watching men in funny clothes queueing up at the well, to draw buckets of water for their thirsty beasts.

Many of them had come a long way, and wanted to stay the night before tackling the long journey home. Mr. and Mrs. Boss were all of a bustle, trying to find room for everybody. The tired animals all needed a good night's rest, too, and the stable began to get over-crowded. Of course, the Moochies began to complain.

"All these strangers," they grumbled. "Eating our food and shoving us about." The Moochies were far too big for anyone to shove, but they stood firmly in their own private corner, rumbling with grumbles.

They were interrupted by Rover, one of the dogs, barking – "Come and look! Come and look!" They all hurried out to see some camels tied up in the yard and few of them had ever seen a camel before. Lady Baa, the oldest sheep, had to explain, adding: "They can't help having humps, so don't stare. It's rude!"

"Foreigners!" snorted the Moochies, turning away in disgust.

It was getting late and all the animals had bedded down as best they could, when Neddy, whose long ears were quick to pick up any sound, heard the Boss saying: "No, I'm sorry but we're full up. There's no room at all." Gentle voices answered, as though pleading, but the Boss went on: "No, we're too full already. It's impossible!"

Presently a lantern was lit and dim figures moved towards the stable.

"Look out!" Neddy warned everybody. "There's more coming!"

There was a chorus of protest: "Oh NO! It's impossible!"

"That's what the Boss said, but they're coming all the same."

They were . . . the Boss leading the way with the lantern, followed by a man leading a tired-looking donkey, with a drooping figure on his back.

The Moochies made a noise like distant thunder and nudged each other. Then, not caring who or what they trod on, they lumbered over to the open door and stood there, filling it completely.

"There's no room here!" they snorted defiantly.

"OUT!" said the Boss. "There'll be a lot more room with you two outside."

As they went, Neddy whispered to his friends: "Come on, let's slip out by the back-door. It's a lovely night. Just look at that moon!"

"That's not the moon, silly!" laughed Rover, knowing how short-sighted donkeys are. "It's a star. Biggest star I ever saw!"

Neddy stretched his long ears up towards the star and said: "I hear singing."

"Stars don't sing." Rover chuckled. "It's just the noise from the inn."

But Neddy shook his head. "It's not that sort of noise," he whispered.

Inside the stable the Boss was saying: "I'm afraid that's the best I can do for you except for some clean hay." He forked down a bundle, while the hens cackled at him.

"It's very kind of you," said the stranger. "Mary is tired."

They turned their donkey loose and Neddy watched him having a long drink from a bucket. "You're tired," said Neddy. "Come and sleep on this bracken. Have you come a long way?"

"Yes," sighed the little donkey as he collapsed on the bracken. "A place called Nazareth."

"Never heard of it," Neddy admitted and the other murmured sleepily: "One day the whole world will have heard of it."

Although many animals understand a lot more than humans do, Neddy was puzzled. There was some strange magic in the air that night. Something stranger than magic . . . stronger than magic. Something very special.

For a long time Neddy stood, listening to that distant singing.

It seemed to be coming from overhead . . . somewhere in the region of that extraordinary star and echoing all around the sky. It made Neddy feel very happy and he would have loved to join in, but donkeys can only bray and he knew that was an ugly noise and might disturb the Lady in the stable.

So he kept quiet . . . listening, wondering and feeling so happy, without really knowing why.

The little donkey from Nazareth had been quite right. Nearly two thousand years later, millions of people, all over the world, feel specially excited and happy on Christmas Eve. You do, too . . . don't you? ☆

Mr Wimpy's Colouring Competition

At the Scouts' Annual Summer Fair there was a surprise visitor — Mr. Wimpy arrived! Everyone was **delighted** to see him and he and all the Cubs and Scouts had a brilliant afternoon riding on the dodgems, trying to win a coconut on the coconut-shy, watching the clowns, having a go on the merry-go-round and all the other fun activities and side-shows that were there.

In our picture opposite you will see that Mr. Wimpy also had a go on the helter-skelter — he certainly seems to be having a lot of fun!

By colouring in this picture — as well as you can and in the most appropriate colours — you could win a great prize for you and the whole of your Pack! All you have to do then is complete the coupon below with your name, address and so on and list the three items in this Annual that you enjoyed most. Then cut the whole page out and send it to: The 1990 Cub Scout Annual Competitions, Editorial Department, The Scout Association, Baden-Powell House, Queen's Gate, LONDON SW7 5JS to arrive no later than February 28, 1990.

You could win:

First Prize — £30 for you *plus* dinner for the whole of your Pack* at Mr. Wimpy's nearest branch to you.

Second Prize — £20 for you *plus* dinner for the whole of your Pack* at Mr. Wimpy's nearest branch to you.

Third Prize — *SIX* prizes each of £10 for you *plus* dinner for the whole of your Six** at Mr. Wimpy's nearest branch to you.

The 1990 Cub Scout Annual extends its thanks to Wimpy International for their generous sponsorship of this competition.

*Pack means up to a maximum of 36 Cub Scouts plus 4 Leaders. ** Six means up to 6 Cub Scouts plus 1 Leader.

Don't miss our other great competition on pages 8 and 9 in this Annual – **and remember** you can send both competition entry coupons in the same envelope and we'll sort them out!

To: The 1990 Cub Scout Annual Competitions, Editorial Department, The Scout Association, Baden-Powell House, Queen's Gate, LONDON SW7 5JS.

PLEASE COMPLETE THIS FORM IN BLOCK CAPITAL LETTERS

Name: . . . .

Address: . . . .

. . . . Post code: . . . .

Cub Scout Pack: . . . .

I am: . . . . . . years . . . . months old

(Date of birth: . . . .)

My three favourite features in this Annual were:

First . . . .

Second . . . .

Third . . . .

Cliff Brown's Animal Puzzle Page

THE SILENT HUNTER. ENTER THE NAMES OF THE ANIMALS PICTURED HERE ACROSS THE GRID AND THE NAME OF OUR SILENT HUNTER WILL APPEAR DIAGONALLY.

HOW MANY ANIMALS? STUDY THE CIRCLE OF LETTERS AND SEE HOW MANY DIFFERENT ANIMALS YOU CAN FIND.

GIRAFFERRELEPHANTELOPECCARYAKOALAMBEARATAPIRABBITGERBILLAMANDRILLEOPARDDOGI

SEE IF YOU CAN FIND THE CONTINUOUS BLACK LINE FROM THE TIP OF HIS HORN TO THE TIP OF HIS TAIL.

VOLCANO!

The day was a hot one, as it usually was during August. In the small town of Pompeii, on the shore of the Tyrrhenian Sea, people were going about their normal business with no thought for the sleeping volcano, just a couple of kilometres behind them. It had shown no signs of life during the town's 600 year existence. Life was pleasant. The year, so far, had been a good one — in fact, everything was normal.

Suddenly, around noon, the peace of that morning, August 24 in the year AD 79, was rudely shattered.

Mount Vesuvius had decided it was time to erupt!

A vast, dense black column of fumes and ash shot into the air and spread outwards into a huge cloud. It quickly covered the distance between the mountain and the town and hot cinders and ash began raining down on the prosperous town of Pompeii.

This rain of debris continued for three days without pause and, by the time it had finished, Pompeii was buried under a blanket of volcanic ash and cinders that was about *5 metres* thick. (That's just under 1.75 metres per day or *over 7 centimetres per hour!*) The coastline, too, had altered greatly and the sea was now nearly three kilometres from the town's waterfront and quays.

Most of the population escaped, but many who tried to leave by boat found that their boats quickly filled with ash and cinders and sank beneath them. About 2,000 of the population of 20,000 are thought to have perished.

illustration by Edgar Hodges
picture by J. E. Guest

Volcanic history

Volcanoes are not a recent 'invention'; the Earth's history of volcanic activity is a very long one. Evidence has been found which has been dated, through various accurate scientific processes, to many thousands of millions of years. Volcanic activity has not been limited to specific areas for, as the Earth's crust plates move around and the shapes of continents change, so different areas come to be sited above a 'hot spot' and go through a volcanic period before the relentless movement shifts them away to a quieter place. Indeed, Scotland has been through several such phases and about 325 million years ago (and that is comparatively recent!) a volcano was active on the site where Edinburgh now stands . . . and this was just one of the hundreds of volcanoes that existed in Scotland at that time.

Three types

Volcanoes fall into three categories.

They are said to be *extinct* when they have shown no sign of activity within historical time — this varies around the world for although the Mediterranean region, for instance, has a history of about 10,000 years, known history in the Antarctic only dates back to the turn of the last century. So the term 'historical time' is pretty flexible.

Secondly, they are said to be *dormant* when there is no major volcanic activity, although the vent (which is what the actual opening is called) may give off fumes from time to time and they may become active at any time.

Finally, they can be *active* which, as it implies, means that they have a record of erupting within historical time.

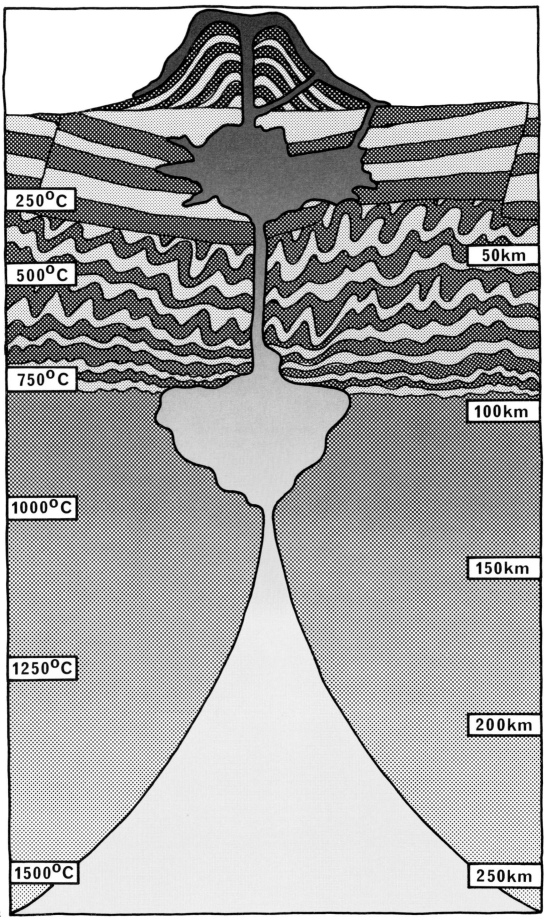

250°C

500°C

750°C

1000°C

1250°C

1500°C

50km

100km

150km

200km

250km

58

A 'new' volcano

A volcano is 'born' when lava (hot liquid rock) breaks through the Earth's surface at a new location. The lava has travelled from below the crust via what is known as a 'volcanic conduit'. This has forced its way through the layers of rock forming the Earth's crust by breaking through the weakest point, so it will not necessarily have followed a straight line. Having broken through the crust, the lava will flow out in all directions and cool. More, still very hot, lava will force its way through this cooling lava and, in its turn, flow out and cool. This continues and first a small hill and then a small mountain will form as layers of lava build up.

The eruption

Some volcanoes have just one vent which they use whenever they choose to erupt. Most, however, have many vents and they tend to open a new vent for each new eruption, so the older the volcano the more vents it is likely to have. This is often caused by the last of the lava from one eruption solidifying in the vent as it cools. Then, when the volcano decides to erupt again, the fresh lava finds that it cannot get out as the vent is blocked by a plug of solid – old – lava so it follows the line of least resistance (which is seldom through the lava above it) and pushes its way out through the sides of the cone – and a new vent is born.

As the lava is making its way down the side of the cone, clouds of gas, vapour and steam rise through the atmosphere, carrying with them ash and cinder. This dense black column has been known to rise thousands of feet into the air. The gas, vapour and steam rise quickly and, through the pull of gravity, the heavier pieces of ash and cinder drop back to Earth. As the temperature of the atmosphere cools the steam it condenses and starts to fall as rain. While this has been happening, the dust and ash have been settling around the cone, forming a thick carpet. When the rain hits this dust deposit it immediately turns to mud, which, when the weight of the rain and dust has built up to the right level, will shoot off downhill at very high speed – speeds of up to 90kph have been recorded. These mud-flows are highly dangerous because of their speed. They are, in fact, far more dangerous and have caused far more destruction and death than lava has. It is a popular misconception that it is the lava which is dangerous – admittedly the lava is exceedingly hot but it moves so slowly that people and animals are able to get out of its way easily. The real menace is the mud-flow.

The lava, travelling very slowly, has been known to flow as far as 80 kilometres from the vent, and it is still so hot that it incinerates or boils everything in its path. So it is only the immovables, like villages, that get caught by lava, people are relatively safe. The lava will retain its heat for many months, sometimes years, as it cools off only very, very slowly.

Answers

Cliff Brown's Communication Puzzle Page
The 'segment' puzzle message reads: Now ask Akela about the real Communication Badge.

Cliff Brown's Musical Puzzle Page
The hidden musical instruments are: saxophone; flute; harmonica; trumpet; violin; cymbal; trombone; tuba; clarinet; guitar; triangle and drum.

The composer is 'Irving Berlin' and he wrote *Alexander's Ragtime Band.*

Jim's confused thoughts showed: tin whistle; jaws harp; concertina; triangle; oboe; trumpet; saxophone; clarinet; harp; violin; mouth organ; horn and recorder.

Cliff Brown's Explorers Puzzle Page
The mixed up signposts were: London – Manchester; Bristol – Aberystwyth; Southampton – Lancaster; Glasgow – Norwich; Blackpool – Folkestone; Nottingham – Basingstoke.

Making FIRE – T I D E
　　　　　　 H I D E
　　　　　　 H I V E
　　　　　　 F I V E
　　　　　　 F I L E
　　　　　　 F I R E

The real detail circles are B, D, F, G, J and K.
The fakes are A, C, E, H, I and L.

Cliff Brown's Animal Puzzle Page
The correct order to enter the animals into the grid was Boar, Camel, Turtle, Lioness, Baboon, Prawn and Seal which produced 'Barn Owl' as the silent hunter.

There were 18 animals to find in the circle. They were, starting from '12 o'clock' and reading clockwise: lamb; bear; rat; tapir; rabbit; tiger; gerbil; llama; mandrill; leopard; dog; giraffe; ferret; elephant; antelope; peccary; yak; koala.

Rhino Puzzle

Action Stations – 3

Fun, games and activities from Norman Garnett and David Easton

More fun with salt

Elsewhere in this book we have told you how to baffle your friends with salt water. Here is another 'trick' using salt and water. You will need some sewing thread, a small curtain ring, some salt, water, a stick and a match. Like all magic tricks, it needs some preparation.

The first thing you need to do is to soak the thread in a strong solution of salt and water. Make the water **very** salty. Soak the thread in it and then hang it up to dry. When it is dry, soak it again and repeat the process three or four times. This can be done the day before you intend to show your trick so that you have plenty of time to give it a number of soakings.

When you are ready to perform, fasten one end of the thread to the ring, and the other end to the stick so that the ring hangs down. You should do this whilst your 'audience' are watching you, and they will not suspect that it is anything other than normal sewing cotton. Hold the stick out, and with your match you light the thread close to the ring.

The flame will spread all the way up the thread, but to everyone's surprise the ring will not fall and the 'thread' will remain intact.

What has really happened, is that the fibres of the thread have burned but a thin tube of salt has survived. This is strong enough to hold the ring.

To do it properly, you have to be most careful not to jerk the stick once you have set fire to the thread. You should also avoid winds or draughts, and it will help if your ring is the lightest you can find.

We had to have three tries before we succeeded – and you will be very lucky if you succeed first time. With this in mind, you should soak more than one piece of thread at a time.

Remember! 'Can't' is a word we never use!

Coin it

Is there someone in your house who collects coins? Here are two games which you can play using a number of coins. You can also use buttons but it is best if they are all the same size. You can also use matches, but playing with matches is always a bit dangerous and you would need to make sure that they were the sort that can only strike on their own box.

Make a line of between 20 and 30 coins or matches. They should be in a straight line, and all touching the one next to them, like this:

Two players play at a time, and they toss up for who starts. Each player takes away one coin at a time EXCEPT that he can take two if they are touching.

Those are the only rules, except for the usual ones about not falling out and not fighting.

The winner is the person who picks up the last coin.

The other game needs just 11 coins. Set them out in rows of 1, 2, 3 and 5. Like this:

Again, for two players, toss up for who goes first.

This time each player can take away as many coins as he wants from one line. You can take a full line if you wish, but you are not allowed to take from more than one line.

The object of the game this time is to leave the last coin for your opponent.

Both of these games need careful thinking about. Always take your time and study your next move.

9-9-9

Why is that policeman sitting up in that tree?
Because he is in Special Branch!

A lorry load of syrup has crashed on the motorway.
The police are asking motorists to stick to the inside lane!

Two bank robbers have crashed into a cement lorry.
The police are searching for two hardened criminals!

A van full of wigs has overturned in high winds.
The police are now combing the area!

A jeweller's shop was robbed in broad daylight. The only witness ran to the police station to tell them all about it. He said that an elephant had run down the street and smashed the window with its tusks, then reached inside with its trunk and stolen a load of jewels, before dashing off at great speed.

"I find that hard to believe," said the sergeant. "Was it an Indian elephant or an African elephant?"

"How do you tell the difference?" asked the witness.

"An Indian elephant has very small ears, but an African elephant has huge ears which flop about. Which sort of ears did this elephant have?" asked the sergeant.

"How do I know?" said the witness. "It was wearing a stocking mask over its head."

Can't

My granny always used to say that "Can't" is a little word you should never use.

When you say "I can't", you usually mean "I don't want to", or "I haven't tried", or even "I am not interested".

However, there are a few things which look very easy but which seem almost impossible when you come to try them.

"You can do anything if you try hard enough," my granny would say. Well, she was wrong, of course. You certainly can't put your left elbow in your left hand. And have you ever tried scratching a wooden leg until it hurts?

Here are one or two teasers which you might care to try. Don't give up easily. And don't say "I can't".

Stand flat against a wall, with your heels touching the wall. Get someone to place a penny at the side of your feet and then try to pick it up without moving your feet.

Get yourself a pencil and a notepad. Hold the pencil in the hand that you normally write with, and the notebook in the other.

Stand up. Lift off the floor the foot which is on the same side as the pencil, and slowly make circles with that foot. If you are standing on your left leg, you will be making circles with your right foot and your foot should move clockwise. If your are standing on your right foot, you will be waving your left foot about and it should go anti-clockwise. That is quite easy so far, and you should keep doing that until you have got a nice easy rhythm going.

All you have got to do now is to draw a large figure 8 on the notepad without stopping your foot from going round in circles.

No matter what my granny used to say, I will bet that you can't do it!

A fishy tale

A sardine fish
is small and thin
and fits inside
a sardine tin

A shark is big
and never fits
unless it's chopped
in smaller bits.

Doug Macleod

Make your own Dustbinbag Kite

with Peter Honeycombe
illustrated by Colin Smale

More correctly known as a 'Grau Sledge', this kite is quick and easy to make, doesn't cost a lot of money, folds up neatly yet flies easily in the lightest of breezes.

You will need:

1 large polythene refuse sack
2 dowel rods, 5mm diameter
  and 90cm long
1 inch wide sticky tape
  (preferably waterproof)
3 metres of cord for the bridle
1 curtain ring
String or cord for flying

What to do:

Slit down one side and cut off the bottom weld of the sack. Lay it flat and mark out the shape and air holes according to the measurements. (*Tip:* Ask Dad to give you some help with this part as the polythene is a bit slippery and you always seem to need at least one more hand!) Cut out the kite with scissors, being careful to get neat corners on the air holes to prevent them tearing when your kite is flying.

Lay the dowel rods on the kite from top to bottom and, using about 10cm lengths of tape, stick them to the polythene in the places indicated. Wrap the tape over the rods and fold it over the edges of the plastic at the top and bottom sides to get a really strong fixing.

Use the tape to reinforce the 'ears' of the kite and make two small holes to attach the bridle. If you can get an eyelet fitted here (or should it be called an 'earlet'?) it will help to keep this part strong.

The bridle is tied to the ears, through the holes, and the curtain ring attached to the exact centre simply by passing the loop through and over the ring.

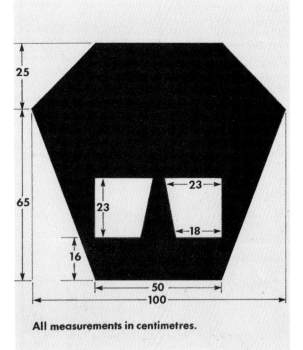

All measurements in centimetres.

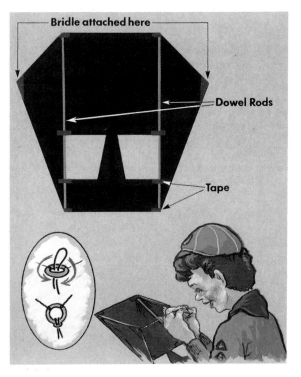

Bridle attached here
Dowel Rods
Tape

This kite almost flies itself. Tie the flying string to the ring (a round turn and two half hitches of course), stand with your back to the wind with the dowel rods facing you. Most times it will take off as soon as you let go.

Remember, you must not fly a kite more than 60 metres above ground level or within 5 kilometers of an airfield, and never, never, near electricity power lines.